Mary Wollstonecraft

Letters to Imlay

With Prefatory Memoir by C. Kegan Paul

Mary Wollstonecraft

Letters to Imlay
With Prefatory Memoir by C. Kegan Paul

ISBN/EAN: 9783744687959

Printed in Europe, USA, Canada, Australia, Japan

Cover: Foto ©Thomas Meinert / pixelio.de

More available books at **www.hansebooks.com**

MARY WOLLSTONECRAFT

*LETTERS TO IMLAY,
WITH PREFATORY MEMOIR BY
C. KEGAN PAUL.*

LONDON:
C. KEGAN PAUL & CO., 1, PATERNOSTER SQUARE.
1879.

CONTENTS.

	PAGE
PREFATORY MEMOIR	v
LETTERS TO IMLAY	1

ETCHINGS.

FROM PORTRAIT IN POSSESSION OF SIR PERCY
F. SHELLEY, BART. . . . . . . *To face Title*

FROM PORTRAIT IN POSSESSION OF WILLIAM
RUSSELL, ESQ. . . . . . . *To face page* 1

*** In giving reproductions of both the portraits by Opie, bearing the name of Mary Wollstonecraft, a word is necessary in reference to some of the difficulties which they present.

The portrait etched for the frontispiece is beyond all doubt that painted by Opie for Godwin during the few months of his marriage with Mary Wollstonecraft, and very shortly before her death. It is now in the possession of Sir Percy Shelley, a direct heirloom from his grandfather, William Godwin. The hair in this portrait is a bright auburn, and corresponds in colour with that cut from Mary Wollstonecraft's head after death. A considerable quantity of this hair is also in Sir Percy Shelley's keeping. The features of the portrait correspond in every degree with a cast taken from the face after death, and show that the likeness must have been as striking as the painting is excellent. It was first engraved, as by Opie, by Heath in 1798, and was published by Johnson, Mary Wollstonecraft's publisher and intimate friend.

The second portrait is in the possession of Mr. William Russell, and was sold to him twenty years since as by Northcote, but was immediately pronounced by him to be by Opie, a fact now certain.

Is it Mary Wollstonecraft?

The face is older, though the likeness to the other portrait is strong. The hair is grey or powdered, the first being impossible in Mary's case, the second unlikely. But it was engraved, as by Opie, by Ridley, and published by Bellamy for the proprietors of the *Monthly Mirror* in 1796, with the name 'Mrs. Wollstonecraft,' that is to say in Mary Wollstonecraft's lifetime, and it does not seem that any doubt was thrown upon it. It is, however, clear from an article in the *Monthly Mirror*, that the print was issued without authority.

There is here a difficulty which is to me quite unsoluble, and I can only leave the puzzle as I find it, saying simply that the authenticity of the first portrait is obviously indisputable, while it is not easy to dispute that of the second.

C. K. P.

MEMOIR.

THE name of Mary Wollstonecraft has long been a mark for obloquy and scorn. Living and dying as a Christian, she has been called an atheist, always a hard name, but harder still some years ago. She ran counter to the customs of society, yet not wantonly or lightly, but with forethought, in order to carry out a moral theory gravely and religiously adopted. Her opinions, save on one point, were those which most cultivated women now hold. Mary Wollstonecraft loved much and suffered much; she had the real enthusiasm of humanity before the words were known which designate a feeling still far from common; and, like many more who think always of others rather than self, she has been one of the martyrs of society. Nor did she win, like some other such martyrs, any immediate recognition when her sufferings ceased in rest, nor had she a certain pride in her rejection while here. She did not carry about in men's sight, as has been said of Byron—

"The pageant of her bleeding heart."

For the most part her great sorrows were hidden, herself was unrecognised, and her name despised.

Known to and loved by only a very few, her writings have been almost unread, the facts of her life ignored, and only eighty years after her death has any serious attempt been made to set her right in the eyes of those who will choose to see her as she was. As the wife of Godwin, her life found place in a memoir of the philosopher published by me in 1876. How completely ignored she has been may be judged from the fact that when Miss Yonge, the well-known authoress of *The Heir of Redcliffe*, prepared some few years since a new edition of *The Elements of Morality*, a book for children, translated by Mary Wollstonecraft from the German, she did not even take the trouble to discover the right name of her whose work she was reproducing, and spelt it *Wolstoncroft* and *Woolstoncroft*.

The following pages reproduce in part, and in part supplement, what was said in my Life of Godwin, in order to do justice to the memory of a woman as good as she was fair, and lovable as she was unfortunate.

Mary Wollstonecraft was born at Hoxton on April 27, 1759. Her father had once been rich, the son of a respectable manufacturer in Spitalfields who had realised a considerable fortune. The family was originally Irish; and Wollstonecraft the younger married an Irishwoman of good family, Elizabeth Dixon.

Never bred to any profession, Mr. Wollstonecraft, when he had spent great part of his patrimony in drink, tried farming, an occupation in which shrewdness, vigilance, and early hours are, above all things, requisite. He got into deeper difficulties, and began a wandering, shifty life, marking each change of residence by a deeper fall in poverty and disrepute. The family roamed from Hoxton to Edmonton, to Essex, to Beverley in Yorkshire, to Laugharne in Pembrokeshire, where he seems to have had some little property, and back to London again.

Mrs. Wollstonecraft died in 1780, leaving six children: Edward, an attorney, in business near the Tower; Mary, Everina, and Eliza; James, who went into the Navy; Charles, who finally emigrated to America. There are some of the name now settled in Australia. I am unable to say of which son they are the descendants.

Mr. Wollstonecraft soon married again; and his wife appears to have done what she could, but quite in vain, to keep him steady and respectable. His home became no fit place for his daughters, and, indeed, the circumstances of the family drove them out to endeavour to earn a livelihood.

The sisters were all clever women, Mary and Eliza far above the average; but their opportunities of culture had been few. They all had a real desire to learn, and were fair French scholars. They all, therefore, turned their thoughts towards teaching, as a profession; and Mary, the eldest, was to make the venture first. In the meantime she went to live with her friend, Fanny Blood, a girl of her own age, whose home life was also unhappy, whose father was much such another as Mr. Wollstonecraft. Fanny Blood was an artist, and supported her family by her profession, or nearly did so, for Mrs. Blood gained a small sum by taking in needlework, in which, so long as they lived together, Mary aided her. Everina went to keep house for Edward; and Eliza made a hasty marriage with Mr. Bishop, in order, it may be supposed, to escape from the shame of her home life and the irksomeness of a teacher's career.

I am not able to discover what position in life Mr. Bishop held: he was, however, what is called a gentleman, and I have some notion he was a clergyman. The marriage was from the first unhappy. It is more than probable there were faults on both sides. All the Wollstonecraft sisters were enthusiastic, excitable, and hasty tempered, apt to exaggerate trifles, sensitive to magnify inattention into slights, and slights into studied insults. All had ill health of a kind which is especially trying to the nerves; and Eliza had, in excess, the family temperament and constitution. She had little actual education, she was very young and inexperienced—scarcely more than seventeen, I take it—at the date of her marriage, so that there was little to counteract the waywardness of a hasty disposition. Yet there can be no doubt, on the other hand, that Bishop was a man of the most furious violence; and this, the third married home which Mary knew intimately, was far worse than even that of her own parents or of the Bloods.

Mary, much attached to her family, was devoted to Eliza, and considered no sacrifice too great to make for her. To save her from misery she gave up all hopes of an independent career, and offered a home to her sister, whom she urged to leave her husband, and, when Mrs. Bishop's reason all but gave way under her trials, arranged her secret and sudden flight.

It was the first occasion on which any of the great social questions presented themselves to Mary Wollstonecraft: but her rapid mind had no hesitation how this one should be answered. Bishop had dissolved his marriage by his brutality, whether temporary laws still held his wife to him or no. Many years afterwards, Mary wrote a sketch, and worked out in detail some chapters, of a story called *The Wrongs of Woman*, but it was still unfinished when she died. Most of the painful scenes in it are simple transcriptions of what she had known and witnessed in her sister's married life; and the root idea of the whole book is the gross immorality of laws which hold a woman to a brutal, loveless savage, who keeps none of those promises on the strength of which the marriage contract has been undertaken.

Mrs. Bishop was in hiding from her husband for some time; but a legal separation—no more was possible—was at last arranged, and the sisters, with Fanny Blood, took a house together. The scheme proposed was that Mary and Eliza should obtain daily pupils, while Fanny should maintain herself as an artist. Their school existed for a while at Newington Green: some influential friends sent them about twenty day scholars; some boarders, two ladies and their children, came to live with them. But the board was irregularly paid; the original want of capital hampered the sisters; and, after languishing for two years, the school expired.

Fanny Blood married, during that time, Mr. Hugh Skeys, a merchant, and went with him to Lisbon. There she died in childbed, having sent for Mary to nurse her, but she only arrived in time to close the eyes of her friend. The first romance which Mary ever wrote, and published a year or two afterwards, was founded on her recollection of this dear companion.

During the period we have now traversed, which brings us to the summer of 1787, when Mary was twenty-eight, she was a voluminous but not a very remarkable letter-writer, and she had written nothing else. Her letters are, save in one point, mainly interesting for the vivid pictures they give of the miserable home life, making the whole family, the Bishops, the Bloods, and others, live again before us. I must, however, venture to refer those who wish to read them, or at least the most interesting of them, to the Life of Godwin before mentioned.

The one point in which they are all specially remarkable is the line they take about religion. It must be remembered that this woman is one accused of having set religion at defiance, and therefore it is that I lay such stress on certain passages. In the same letter in which she has written to Everina that, on her advice and her responsibility, Mrs. Bishop was to leave her husband for ever, and in which she recognises that she is flying in the face of all received traditions by giving such counsel, she says:

> Don't suppose I am preaching when I say uniformity of conduct cannot in any degree be expected from those whose first motive of action is not the pleasing the Supreme Being; and those who humbly rely on Providence will not only be supported in affliction, but have a peace imparted to them that is past all describing. This state is indeed a warfare, and we have little that we don't smart for in the attaining. The cant of weak enthusiasts has made the consolations of religion and the assistance of the Holy Spirit appear ridiculous to the inconsiderate, but it is the only solid foundation of comfort that the weak efforts of reason will be assisted, and our hearts and minds corrected and improved, till the time arrives when we shall not only see *perfection*, but every creature around us happy.

Again, to George Blood, Fanny's brother, who had got into a somewhat serious scrape, she writes:

> Do your duty and leave the rest to Heaven; forfeit not that sure support in the time of trouble, and though your want of experience and judgment may betray you into

many errors, let not your heart be corrupted by bad example, and then, though it may be wounded by neglect and torn by anguish, you will not feel that most acute of all sorrows, a sense of having deserved the miseries that you undergo.

Again, to the same :

It gives me the sincerest satisfaction to find that you look for comfort where only it is to be met with, and that Being in whom you trust will not desert you. Be not cast down : while we are struggling with care, life slips away, and through the assistance of Divine grace we are obtaining habits of virtue that will enable us to relish those joys that we cannot now form any idea of. I feel myself particularly attached to those who are heirs of the promises, and travel on in the thorny path with the same Christian hopes that render my severe trials a cause of thankfulness when I can think.

These quotations need not, though they might indefinitely, be multiplied. Nor is the advice given with the unconcerned manner of one who looks on suffering from the outside. Remember that she herself was crying out of the deeps, was walking in the valley of the shadow of death. There have been few more joyless lives—all who surrounded her sordid, sensual, and base—constant ill-health, constant poverty. As Mrs. Browning says of Cowper,

He wore no less a loving face because so broken-hearted,

Mary, while building up her sister and her friend in the faith and in hope, wrote of herself:

My harrassed mind will in time wear out my body. I have been so hunted down by cares, and see so many that I must encounter, that my spirits are quite depressed. I have lost all relish for life, and my almost broken heart is only cheered by the prospect of death. I may be years a-dying though, and so I ought to be patient, for at this time to wish myself away would be selfish.

Again, after Fanny's death :

Could I not look for comfort where only 'tis to be found, I should have been mad before this, but I feel that I am supported by that Being who alone can heal a wounded spirit. May He bless you both.

It is not perhaps unworthy of notice that among the friends gathered round the sisters at Newington, who gained them pupils and aided them with friendly counsel, two out of the three names of men which meet us most often in the letters are those of clergymen.

Through one of these she became acquainted with Mr. Prior, an Assistant Master at Eton, who was commissioned by Lord Kingsborough to find a governess for his daughter. After spending some time at Eton she travelled to Ireland with her hosts, and entered on her duties as governess to the Misses King in October, 1787, at a salary of £40 a year. Her sisters obtained various situations of the same kind which need not here be particularised.

It was singularly unfortunate that Mary Wollstonecraft was fated, as it were, to see the unattractive side of almost all the great institutions of society with which she was brought into contact: marriage, education, particularly religious education as administered at Eton, and aristocratic life. When she afterwards wrote her *Vindication of The Rights of Woman* her views on all these subjects were coloured by her own personal experiences. Like all women and most men, she generalised from particulars, and never suspected that such a one-sided view must be partially unfair.

The language which she uses of Eton is probably not too severe, and the points on which she animadverts are not exaggerated: the fine of a guinea for non-attendance at certain religious rites was still in existence, if not at Eton, yet in several Oxford colleges, even in my own recollection.

At boarding schools of every description (she writes) the relaxation of the junior boys is mischief; and of the senior vice. Besides, in great schools, what can be more prejudicial to the moral character than the system of tyranny and abject slavery which is established among the boys, to say nothing of the slavery to forms, which makes religion worse than a farce? For what good can be expected from the youth who receives the sacrament of the Lord's Supper to avoid forfeiting a guinea, which he probably afterwards spends in some sensual manner?

Nothing, indeed, can be more irreverent than the cathedral service as it is now performed in this country, neither does it contain a set of weaker men than those who are the slaves of this childish routine. A disgusting skeleton of the former state is still exhibited, but all the solemnity that interested the imagination, if it did not purify the heart, is stripped off. The performance of high mass on the Continent must impress every mind where a spark of fancy glows, with that awful melancholy, that sublime tenderness, so near akin to devotion. I do not say that these devotional feelings are of more use in a moral sense than any other question of taste, but I contend that the theatrical pomp which gratifies our senses is to be preferred to the cold parade which insults the understanding without reaching the heart.

The remarks on the teachers and the teaching are quite as severe, and, I take it, not less deserved.

The society which she found in Ireland was scarcely more congenial. Lord Kingsborough, afterwards Earl of Kingston, was a coarse, hearty, jovial, but not unkindly country squire; Lady Kingsborough, a mere fine lady, without true refinement. One child only among her charges specially attracted her, "dear Margaret," as she is called in the letters, afterwards Lady Mountcashel. This lady's own after-life was sad, nor was her character free from blame. It is therefore necessary once more to draw attention to Mary Wollstonecraft's own earnest orthodox piety, and the high morality which runs through all her letters. For one of the chief slanders brought against the governess in long-after days was that she had corrupted the minds of her pupils, teaching them base morality and false religion. On the contrary, her whole endeavour was to train them for higher pursuits, and to instil into them a desire for a wider culture than fell to the lot of most girls in those days. Her sorrow was deep that her pupils' lives were such as to render sustained study and religious habits of mind alike difficult. Most of the women with whom Mary Wollstonecraft came in contact were frivolous, and most of the men were coarse. It is not wonderful that her spirits flagged, and in spite of the affection of the one child to whom she was attracted, she saw almost everything around her in gloomy colours.

After a year's sojourn in Ireland Lady Kingston dismissed her governess because—the reason was distinctly avowed—the children loved the governess more than their mother, and the latter became jealous.

The promise of literary skill which Mary had shown before she left London, and a little tale called *Mary*, written during her year in Ireland, induced Mr. Johnson, the publisher in St. Paul's Churchyard, to offer her constant literary work, mainly in the way of translation from the French.

She also acted as Mr. Johnson's literary adviser or "reader," and the following letter to Miss Hayes in regard to the preface of a volume of Essays was written in this capacity. Her honest plainness of speech on this occasion, led to a long friendship, which had, as will be seen, memorable influence on her after life.

> I yesterday mentioned to Mr. Johnson your request, and he assented, desiring that the title page might be sent to him. I therefore can say nothing more, for trifles of this kind I have always left to him to settle; and, you must be aware, madam, that the *honour* of publishing, the phrase on which you have laid a stress, is the cant of both trade and sex: for if really equality should ever

take place in society, the man who is employed and gives a just equivalent for the money he receives will not behave with the servile obsequiousness of a servant.

I am now going to treat you with still greater frankness. I do not approve of your preface—and I will tell you why. If your work should deserve attention, it is a blur on the very face of it. Disadvantages of education, &c., ought, in my opinion, never to be pleaded with the public in excuse for defects of any importance, because if the writer has not sufficient strength of mind to overcome the common difficulties which lie in his way, nature seems to command him, with a very audible voice, to leave the task of instructing others to those who can. This kind of vain humility has ever disgusted me—and I should say to an author, who humbly sued for forbearance, If you have not a tolerably good opinion of your own production, why intrude it on the public? We have plenty of bad books already, that have just gasped for breath and died. The last paragraph I particularly object to—it is so full of vanity. Your male friends will still treat you like a woman—and many a man, for instance Dr. Johnson, Lord Littleton, and even Dr. Priestley have insensibly been led to utter warm eulogiums in private that they would be sorry openly to avow without some cooling explanatory ifs. An author, especially a woman, should be cautious lest she too hastily swallows the crude praises which partial friend and polite acquaintance bestow thoughtlessly when the supplicating eye looks for them. In short, it requires great resolution to try rather to be useful than to please. With this remark in your head, I must beg you to pardon my freedom whilst you consider the purport of what I am going to add—rest on yourself. If your essays have merit, they will stand alone, if not, the *shouldering up* of Dr. this or that will not long keep them from falling to the ground. The vulgar have a pertinent proverb—" Too many cooks spoil the broth ; " and let me remind you that when weakness claims indulgence, it seems to justify the despotism of strength. Indeed, the preface, and even your pamphlet, is too full of yourself— inquiries ought to be made before they are answered ; and till a work strongly interests the public, true modesty should keep the author in the back ground—for it is only about the character and life of a *good* author that curiosity is active—a blossom is but a blossom.

Nov. 25th, 1792.

St. Paul's.—As you seemed uneasy when you wrote, contrary to my first intention, I have just now spoken to Mr. J., who desires me to tell you that he very willingly waves the privilege of seniority, though as it is an impropriety, I should think his name might as well be omitted.

While working in this manner for Mr. Johnson, Mary lived in lodgings in George Street, close to Blackfriars Bridge, and worked hard in this employ for five years, finding places for her sisters, and giving them a home when they needed one. Out of her slender earnings she sent Everina to France. Mr. Johnson lived above his business premises, and saw much literary society, among which Mary was always welcome. It is amusing to find that she made a friend of Mrs. Trimmer, whom she calls "a truly respectable woman." During this period she translated, among many other books, *Lavater's Physiognomy;* wrote for children *Original Stories from Real Life,* now, perhaps, best known by Blake's striking illustrations; and last, but not least, *A Vindication of the Rights of Woman.*

This work is one which has ever been more known by name than by perusal, and it is written on a subject which even now excites acrimony rather than calm discussion. The very words "A Vindication of the Rights of Woman" are held, without examination, to claim emancipation, alike from law, from custom, and from morality. Yet it is evident that the writer, as she has shown herself in her letters, must have changed far more suddenly than is wont to be the case, if such indeed was the object she set before her in writing the treatise.

It is not among the least oddities of this singular work that it is dedicated "to M. Talleyrand-Périgord, late Bishop of Autun." Mary Wollstonecraft, always confiding and always charitable, still believed in him. She little knew how unstable was the liberalism for which she gave him credit, and though well aware that some of her opinions were opposed to those which Talleyrand had put forward in his pamphlet on National Education, she yet thought him sincere.

Mary Wollstonecraft, like so many others, turned to France as the land from which was rising the day-star of a new time; yet, unlike many others, she was far from considering that all French manners were worthy of imitation. Even in the dedication to Talleyrand are some noble words in defence of English cleanliness in life and talk, even of seeming prudery, rather than much which is still tolerated in France.

In the dedication she states the "main argument" of the work, "built on this simple principle, that if woman be not prepared by education to become the companion of man, she will stop the progress of knowledge, for truth must be common to all, or it will be inefficacious with respect to its influence on general practice."

In carrying out this argument the most noticeable fact is the extraordinary plainness of speech, and this it was that caused all or nearly all the outcry. For Mary Wollstonecraft did not, as has been supposed, attack the institution of marriage; she did not assail orthodox religion, she did not even directly claim much which at the present day is claimed by the most moderate Liberals for women and their work. She says :—

> I respect marriage as the foundation of almost every social virtue. Religion, (she exclaims in another place,) pure source of comfort in this vale of tears! how has thy clear stream been muddled by the dabblers who

have presumptuously endeavoured to confine in one narrow channel the living waters that ever flow towards God, the sublime ocean of existence! What would life be without that peace which the love of God, built on humanity, alone can impart? Every earthly affection turns back at intervals to prey upon the heart that feeds it, and the purest effusions of benevolence, often rudely damped by man, must mount as a free-will offering to Him who gave them birth, whose bright image they faintly reflect.

The book was really a plea for equality of education, passing into one for State education, and for the joint education of the sexes, which some of us now again strongly uphold, and which has been, in some instances, tried with marked success. It was a protest against woman being deemed only the plaything of man, an assertion that intellectual companionship was the chief as it is the lasting happiness of marriage. In maintaining these theses, she assailed the theories not only of Rousseau in *Emile*, which would have been easily forgiven her, but those of Dr. Fordyce, whose sermons had long made a part of a young woman's library, of Dr. Gregory, and others, whose words were as a gospel to the average English matron. She did but carry out what Day had sketched in *Sandford and Merton* almost without blame.

It may, however, be admitted that her frankness on some subjects not usually discussed in print, is little less than astounding, while side blows are administered to much which was then unquestioned. The fallacy by which virtue is confounded with reputation is laid bare, and she by no means shrinks from uncovering the worst sores of society. She dealt directly with dangerous and explosive subjects, incidentally upheld greater freedom of divorce, and denied the eternity of the torments of hell.

It was not only the plain speaking which alarmed, not only that a woman spoke, but every page showed that she too was affected by the thoughts which claimed rights for Man, and the demand for these rights was even then issuing in the French Revolution.

The book has grave faults, besides those necessarily incident to the time, but its merits are great also; there is much that is valuable for these days—it is fresh, vigorous, eloquent; it should ever be remembered, if not read, as the herald of the demand that woman should be the equal and the friend, not the slave and toy of man. I will quote as a specimen of her sarcastic vehemence the concluding passage of this memorable book :

Let woman share the rights, and she will emulate the virtues of man; for she must grow more perfect when emancipated, or justify the authority that chains such a weak being to her duty. If the latter, it will be expedient to open a fresh trade with Russia for whips; a present which a father should always make to his son-in-law on his wedding-day, that a husband may keep his whole family in order by the same means; and without any violation of justice reign, wielding this sceptre, sole master of his house, because he is the only being in it who has reason—the Divine indefeasible earthly sovereignty breathed into man by the Master of the Universe. Allowing this position, women have not any inherent rights to claim, and, by the same rule, their duties vanish, for rights and duties are inseparable.

Be just then, O ye men of understanding! and mark

not more severely what women do amiss than the vicious tricks of the horse or the ass for whom ye provide provender, and allow her the privileges of ignorance, to whom ye deny the rights of reason, or ye will be worse than Egyptian taskmasters, expecting virtue where nature has not given understanding !

Among those most scandalised by the publication of the work were Mrs. Bishop and Everina Wollstonecraft. It is not surprising that they did not agree with the views contained in it, but the small spite with which it is discussed in their letters which still remain seems to point to envy and jealousy far more than to honest indignation at opinions. The sisters were both in situations, and in a degree independent of Mary's pecuniary aid. She did less for them since they needed less, more for her own culture, and more for her needy and, it must be added, worthless brother Charles. These were sins which jealous and petty natures could neither overlook nor forgive.

Mrs. Wollstonecraft, for such was the brevet rank she took after the publication of her book, determined to go to France for a few weeks; her book had been translated into French, she wished to see the Revolution at, as it then seemed, its peaceful work, and to perfect her French accent; her scholarship was already excellent. The party was to consist of Mr. Johnson, Mr. and Mrs. Fuseli, and herself, but the others were prevented going, and Mary went alone to Paris in December, 1792, boarding at the house of Madame Filliettaz, *née* Bregantz, a lady in whose school at Putney Mrs. Bishop and Everina had been teachers.

Mr. and Mrs. Fuseli had long been friends of Mary, and slander attempted in after years to make out an attachment between her and Fuseli, which stuck sufficiently to make even Godwin surmise that had Fuseli been free, Mary might have been in love with him. But in fact Godwin knew extremely little of his wife's earlier life, nor was this a subject on which he had sought enlightenment from herself. I can only here say that I fail to find any confirmation whatever of this preposterous story, as told in Knowles's *Life of Fuseli*, or in any other form, while I find much which makes directly against it, the strongest fact being that Mary remained to the end the correspondent and close friend of Mrs. Fuseli.

She went to Paris heart-whole, having reached the age of thirty-five without, so far as I can discover, any trace of a romance such as comes into most women's lives at a far earlier period. Were it not that her life had been so lonely, that her gentlemen friends had been staid elderly persons, who stood to her in the light of father or elder brothers, this might seem strange in the case of one so gifted and so fair.

Like her mind, however, her beauty would appear to have ripened late. In July, 1792, Mrs. Bishop says in a letter to Everina that Charles informs her "that Mrs. Wollstonecraft had grown quite handsome." The grudging admission is more than confirmed by her portrait by Opie, now in the possession of Sir

Percy Shelley, which is the first in this volume, and which was painted for Godwin during the brief period of her marriage; long therefore after she had reached mature age, and when all the waves and storms of her sorrows had gone over her. More than one print was engraved of that portrait, in which is well preserved its tender, wistful, childlike, pathetic beauty, with a look of pleading against the hardness of the world, which I know in one only other face, that of Beatrice Cenci. But those prints can give no notion of the complexion, rich, full, healthy, vivid, of the clear brown eyes, and masses of brownish auburn hair. The fault of the face was that one eyelid slightly drooped. In spite of this defect Southey speaks of her eyes as the most meaning he ever saw, though he did not quite like an expression on her features "indicating superiority," whatever that may imply, for he says it was not haughtiness or sarcasm.

Such was Mary Wollstonecraft when she

landed in France. She had very good introductions, amongst others to Helen Maria Williams, the author, great-aunt to the late distinguished Athanase Coquerel. A few days after her arrival she saw one of the memorable scenes of the Revolution, and described it in words worthy of its unique character. She thus narrates the passage of the King to his trial in a letter to Mr. Johnson:

About nine o'clock this morning (Dec. 26, 1792) the King passed by my window, moving silently along—excepting now and then a few strokes on the drum, which rendered the stillness more awful—through empty streets, surrounded by the National Guards, who, clustering round the carriage, seemed to deserve their name. The inhabitants flocked to their windows, but the casements were all shut; not a voice was heard, nor did I see anything like an insulting gesture. For the first time since I entered France I bowed to the majesty of the people, and respected the propriety of behaviour, so perfectly in unison with my own feelings. I can scarcely tell you why, but an association of ideas made the tears flow insensibly from my eyes, when I saw Louis, sitting with more dignity than I expected from his character, in a hackney coach, going to meet death where so many of his race have triumphed. My fancy instantly brought Louis XIV. before me, entering the capital with all his pomp, after one of the victories most flattering to his pride, only to see the sunshine of prosperity overshadowed by the sublime gloom of misery. I have been alone ever since, and though my mind is calm, I cannot dismiss the lively images that have filled my imagination all the day. Nay, do not smile, but pity me; for once or twice, lifting my eyes from the paper, I have seen eyes glare through a glass door opposite my chair, and bloody hands shook at me. Not the distant sound of a footstep can I hear. My apartments are remote from those of the servants, the only persons who sleep with me in an immense hotel, one folding-door opening after another. I wish I had even kept the cat with me! I want to see something alive; death, in so many frightful shapes, has taken hold of my fancy. I am going to bed, and for the first time in my life I cannot put out the candle.

We all remember that within a month the king, whom Mary saw and pitied, went on a sadder journey still. On January 21, 1793, Louis was beheaded, and before the first week of March had ended all diplomatic relations were over between England and France—the two countries were at war. "The coalised kings threaten us," said Danton; "we hurl at their feet, as gage of battle, the head of a king."

Unless Mary had gone at once, she could not

go away at all. From the date of the king's death the position of every English resident in France became extremely hazardous. The hatred against the countrymen and the countrywomen of Pitt can scarcely be imagined in these calmer times; and Paris, always cruel in panic, was soon in the throes of what has been so well called "The Terror." Want was added to personal danger in the case of many residents; crowds assembled in the streets, clamouring for the barest needs of life, *du pain et du savon*—for bread and soap.

Mary shared to the full this want and difficulty. It was impossible for her to communicate with her sisters, or to receive remittances from England. The letter to Mr. Johnson was the last tidings of her for more than eighteen months.

The American community in Paris did not of course share the suspicion, dislike, and danger which were the lot of the English. One of these Americans, Captain Gilbert Imlay, became acquainted with Mary in the spring of 1793.

After he left the American army, on the conclusion of peace, he became a commissioner for laying out land in the back settlements. From Kentucky he wrote letters on the state of the country to an Irish friend, who published them in Dublin in 1793. Though they were written *currente calamo*, and had not the advantage of the writer's final revision, the *Topographical Description of the Western Territory of North America* is a model of what a monograph on a new country should be. It is at once clear, full, and condensed, is even now interesting, and in its own day went through many editions. Its language throughout shows an educated, accomplished man.

Imlay had now entered into various commercial speculations, of which the centre appears to have been Havre, and his trade was with Norway and Sweden, presumably in timber, since that industry had mainly attracted him in

America. At the time of which we speak he was successful in commerce, and he had considerable command of money. The kindness he showed Mary Wollstonecraft disposed her to look on him favourably; she soon gave him a very sincere affection, and consented to become his wife.

I use this word deliberately, although no legal ceremony ever passed between them. Her view was that a common affection was marriage, and that the marriage tie should not bind after the death of love, if love should die. It is probable, however, that, like many others who hold the same views, only a series of untoward circumstances made her act upon her opinions. A legal marriage with Imlay was certainly difficult, apparently impossible. Her position as a British subject was full of danger—a marriage would have forced her openly to declare herself as such. It is a strong confirmation of the view here taken to find that Madame de Stael, who, if any one, knew the period of which we are speaking, makes a like fact the sole obstacle to the marriage of Lord Nelvil and Madame d'Arbigny. She says:

> Je l'aurais épousée, comme elle le voulait, s'il ne se fût pas rencontré dans ce moment les plus grands obstacles à ce qu'un Anglais pût se marier en France, en déclarant, comme il le fallait, son nom à l'officier civil.—" Corinne, ou l'Italie," Vol. II., p. 63. 8th Edition. Paris, 1818.

It may be doubted whether the ceremony, if any could have taken place, would have been valid in England. Passing as Imlay's wife, without such preparatory declaration, her safety was assured, and as his wife she was acknowledged by him. Charles Wollstonecraft wrote from Philadelphia that he had seen a gentleman who knew his sister in Paris, and that he was "informed that she is married to Captain Imlay of this country."

Long after the period at which we have now arrived, when Imlay's affection had ceased, and his desertion of Mary had practically begun, he entrusted certain important business negotiations to her, and speaks of her in a legal document as "Mary Imlay, my best friend and wife," a document which in many cases and countries would be considered as constituting a marriage. She believed that his love, which was to her sacred, would endure. No one can read her letters without seeing that she was a pure, high-minded, and refined woman, and that she considered herself, in the eyes of God and man, Imlay's wife. Religious as she was and with a strong moral sense, she yet made the grand mistake of supposing that it is possible for one woman to undo the consecrated custom of ages, to set herself in opposition to the course of society, and not be crushed by it. And she made the no less fatal mistake of judging Imlay by her own standard, and thinking that he was as true, as impassioned, as self-denying as herself.

Mary Wollstonecraft was living with Imlay as his wife in Paris in August, 1793, when he was called to Havre on business, and was absent for some months. During this period began the series of letters written to Imlay, which were given up to her on their final separation, and which were first published after her death. "They are," as Godwin said of them, "the offspring of a glowing imagination, and a heart penetrated with the passion it essays to describe." But the earlier letters of the series are also those of a tender and devoted wife, who feels no doubt of her position. Towards the close of 1793 Mary joined Imlay at Havre, and there in the spring of 1794 gave birth to a girl, who received the name of Fanny, in memory of the dear friend of her youth.

At Havre, as before in Paris, she was left much alone, and turned again eagerly to literary work. She wrote at this time a book which is almost unknown, but which well deserves recognition, under the somewhat ambitious title of *An Historical and Moral View of the Origin and Progress of the French Revolution, and the Effect it has produced in Europe.* She intended to complete this in three or four volumes, but only one was published, and went almost immediately through two editions.

It brings the history of the Revolution down to the time of the King's removal to Paris, and therefore includes the taking of the Bastille, the march of the women on Versailles, and other dramatic occurrences, which we all know so well in the graphic pages of Carlyle. But she also goes carefully into the whole state of society and politics, and into the causes of the Revolution, in a most masterly way; her remarks are throughout characterised by a singular moderation, and the work is, I think, the best balanced and most philosophical book on the Revolution, as far as it had then gone.

It has the great advantage that the writer lived and preserved her calmness through so much of what she describes, and it is strangely little coloured by the fleeting opinion of the time. Some hard words, some very strong epithets, are indeed used of Marie Antoinette, showing that she who could in those matters know nothing personally, could not but depend on Paris gossip; but this is interesting, as showing what the view taken of the Queen was before passion rose to its highest, before the fury of the people, with all the ferocity of word and deed attendant on great popular movements, had broken out. May we not say that probably the truth lies between Burke's sparkling eloquence and Carlyle's enthusiastic exclamations on the one side, and on the other the scurrilous insinuations of the mob about the fêtes at the Trianon?

Her accounts of the Bastille siege, and of the Versailles episode, are worth reading beside those of the master to whose style they are so great a contrast. Carlyle has seized on the comic element in the march to Versailles, Mary Wollstonecraft on the tragic, and hers seems to me the worthier view.

As an instance of her impartial—may I, remembering what those days were, say masculine judgment, the concluding passage of the volume may be quoted, in which she accounts for, while fully admitting the ferocity of the Revolution.

The only excuse that can be made for the ferocity of the Parisians is then simply to observe that they had not any confidence in the laws, which they had always found to be merely cobwebs to catch small flies. Accustomed to be punished themselves for every trifle, and often for only being in the way of the rich, or their parasites; when in fact had the Parisians seen the execution of a noble or priest, though convicted of crimes beyond the daring of vulgar minds? When justice, or the law, is so partial, the day of retribution will come with the red sky of vengeance, to confound the innocent with the guilty. The mob were barbarous beyond the tiger's cruelty: for how could they trust a Court that had so often deceived them, or expect to see its agents punished, when the same measures were pursuing?

Let us cast our eyes over the history of man, and we shall scarcely find a page that is not tarnished by some foul deed or bloody transaction. Let us examine the catalogue of the vices of men in a savage state, and contrast them with those of men civilized; we shall find that a barbarian, considered as a moral being, is an angel compared with the refined villain of artificial life. Let us investigate the causes which have produced this degeneracy, and we shall discover that they are those unjust plans of government, which have been formed by peculiar circumstances in every part of the globe. Then let us coolly and impartially contemplate the improvements which are gaining ground in the formation of principles of policy; and I flatter myself it will be allowed by every humane and considerate being, that a political system more simple than has hitherto existed, would effectually check those aspiring follies, which, by imitation, leading to vice, have banished from governments the very shadow of justice and magnanimity.

Thus had France grown up and sickened on the corruption of a state diseased. But, as in medicine, there is a species of complaint in the bowels which works its own cure, and, leaving the body healthy, gives an invigorated tone to the system, so there is in politics: and whilst the agitation of its regeneration continues, the excrementitious humours exuding from the contaminated body will excite a general dislike and contempt for the nation; and it is only the philosophical eye, which looks into the nature and weighs the consequences of human actions, that will be able to discern the cause which has produced so many dreadful effects.

From Havre, then called Havre Marat, in lieu of its old name, Le Havre de Grâce, Mary wrote, as soon as she could, to her sisters, quite unconscious of their change of feeling towards her, though her letters insensibly to herself begin to betray a change in her own happiness.

Imlay became involved in a multitude of speculations, which rendered him dissatisfied with the competency hitherto secured, and thoroughly restless. The plan that he and his wife had proposed to themselves was that they should settle in a farm either in France or America, but he now embarked in fresh ventures in Norway, which would, he considered, bring him a large fortune. His interest in Mary and his child sensibly cooled, and though he allowed them to join him in England—he had left them still longer alone at Havre than he had done in Paris—her letters to him show that she went with a heavy heart and gloomy forebodings of coming sorrow. The meeting was but the prelude to another long separation. Imlay's affairs were seriously embarrassed, and although there was no word of a permanent breach, it was evident that trade was, before all things, the main interest in his life, and that nothing was farther from his intentions than to be satisfied with competency, if it might be realised, and to settle down. It proved necessary that some one should go to Sweden and Norway, on Imlay's part, to arrange some business matters, while his own presence was urgently needed elsewhere. The voyage, it was thought, would prove advantageous to Mary's health, and in June, 1795, less than two months after their meeting, she started on her journey.

The document still exists, of which I have already spoken, in which Imlay calls her his wife, and gives her plenary powers to act for him.

Her letters to Imlay during this period were afterwards divested of all that was personal and private, and published under the title *Letters written during a short Residence in Sweden, Norway, and Denmark,* and are a thoroughly picturesque and graceful description of a summer tour.

On her return to England, in the late autumn, she found letters awaiting her from Imlay, which made it plain that he intended to leave her, but offering to settle an annuity on her and her child. For herself she rejected this offer with scorn. "From you," she wrote, "I will not receive any more. I am not sufficiently humbled to depend on your beneficence." They met again, when Imlay attempted to gloss over the past, and it seemed possible that for the child's sake they might still remain together. But though he had assured her that he had no other attachment, she soon discovered that he was carrying on an unworthy intrigue under her own roof. Driven to despair, and for a time quite out of her mind, she attempted to drown herself by leaping from Putney Bridge, and when that attempt was frustrated—although she was quite insensible when she was taken out of the water—she still nursed for awhile the desire of ending her existence.

I do not know how far a great novelist of our day has consciously borrowed the incident, or has adopted it only with the keen insight of genius, but the attempted suicide of Myra, in *Daniel Deronda*, is in its touching details very like that of Mary Wollstonecraft. Mary, before the leap which should have been fatal, walked into the water, and stood there a while; not however in the glory of a summer sunset, which might add a picturesqueness to death, but in the chill fog of a winter's day, in order that her garments might be sufficiently saturated to prevent her instinctive struggles to save herself from the fate she deliberately chose. The unexpected succour given her by some watermen, in a passing boat, long seemed but cruel kindness.

Mr. Johnson, as before, was the most helpful and most cordial among her friends, and aided her once more to support herself by her pen. She thenceforward resented all attempts of Imlay to provide for her—attempts which, as after circumstances proved, were made for the sake of appearances, and not with any cordial reality.

> I want not (she said) such vulgar comfort, nor will I accept it. I never wanted but your heart; that gone, you have nothing more to give. Forgive me if I say that I shall consider any direct or indirect attempt to supply my necessities as an insult I have not merited, and as rather done out of tenderness for your own reputation than for me.

With reference to Fanny's maintenance, she neither accepted nor refused anything. "You must do as you please with regard to the child," was her final decision. Imlay eventually gave a bond for a sum to be settled on his child, the interest to be devoted to her education; but neither principal nor interest was ever paid.

Imlay vanishes thenceforward from our sight, and we care little to endeavour to trace him; it would probably be useless. I have found no mention of his further notice of his daughter, or, if he was still living, of sorrow for her tragic fate in 1816.

In the literary and liberal society among which Mary Wollstonecraft now mixed, Mrs. Reveley, afterwards the Mrs. Gisborne to whom were written Shelley's well-known lines, was, perhaps, her most intimate friend. From her, and from Miss Hayes, Mrs. Shelley in after life heard almost all that she knew of her mother. Miss Hayes was a lady of some little literary fame in her own day, which fame she long survived, dying in 1843, aged eighty-three. At her house Mary Wollstonecraft met William Godwin once or twice before she went to Norway, and there they met again when after her separation from Imlay she went once more into society. I am indebted to the niece of this lady for various interesting letters in her possession.

Godwin wrote as follows to Miss Hayes in answer to her invitation to him to renew the acquaintance :

[*Jan.* 1796].
Tuesday, 11 *o'clock.*

I will do myself the pleasure of waiting on you on Friday, and shall be happy to meet Mrs. Wollstonecraft, of whom I know not that I ever said a word of harm, and who has frequently amused herself with depreciating me. But I trust you acknowledge in me the reality of a habit upon which I pique myself, that I speak of the qualities of others uninfluenced by personal considerations, and am as prompt to do justice to an enemy as to a friend.

From the testimony of these loving friends Mrs. Shelley gives the following picture of her mother. Her note is especially interesting as showing the sympathy, partly intellectual, partly physical, felt by the gifted daughter for the still more gifted mother, who died in giving her birth.

Mary Wollstonecraft (says Mrs. Shelley) was one of those beings who appear once perhaps in a generation to gild humanity with a ray which no difference of opinion nor chance of circumstances can cloud. Her genius was undeniable. She had been bred in the hard school of adversity, and having experienced the sorrows entailed on the poor and the oppressed, an earnest desire was kindled in her to diminish those sorrows. Her sound understanding, her intrepidity, her sensibility and eager sympathy, stamped all her writings with force and truth, and endowed them with a tender charm which enchants while it enlightens. She was one whom all loved who had ever seen her. Many years are passed since that beating heart has been laid in the cold still grave, but no one who has ever seen her speaks of her without enthusiastic veneration. Did she witness an act of injustice, she came boldly forward to point it out and induce its reparation; was there discord between friends or relatives, she stood by the weaker party, and by her earnest appeals and kindliness awoke latent affection, and healed all wounds. "Open as day to melting charity," with a heart brimful of generous affection, yearning for sympathy, she had fallen on evil days, and her life had been one course of hardship, poverty, lonely struggle and bitter disappointment.

Godwin met her at the moment when she was deeply depressed by the ingratitude of one utterly incapable of appreciating her excellence, who had stolen her heart, and availed himself of her excessive and thoughtless generosity to plunge her in difficulties and then desert her. Difficulties, worldly difficulties, indeed, she set at nought, compared with her despair of good, her confidence betrayed ; and when once she could conquer the misery which clung to her heart, she struggled cheerfully to meet the poverty which was her inheritance, and to do her duty by her darling child.

Godwin's first impression of her was not a pleasing one. He wished to hear Tom Paine talk, who was also of the party, and always a silent man, and he thought Mrs. Imlay talked too much. He was also an extremely fastidious critic, and had been offended at some slight verbal inaccuracies, or what seemed to him such, in her earlier works. But after reading the *Letters from Sweden,* his views about her culture were wholly altered. He saw that the blemishes, if indeed they had existed, were but superficial, and he speedily yielded to the charm which all who knew her recognised. She on her side found that she could love again, and an attachment was soon understood between them, though not at once declared to the world. Godwin writes of this period :

The partiality we conceived for each other was in that mode which I have always considered as the purest and most refined style of love. It grew with equal advances in the mind of each. It would have been impossible for the most minute observer to have said who was before and who was after. One sex did not take the priority which long-established custom has awarded it, nor the other overstep that delicacy which is so severely imposed. I am not conscious that either party can assume to have been the agent or the patient, the toil-spreader or the prey in the affair. When in the course of things the disclosure came, there was nothing in a manner for either party to disclose to the other. There was no period of throes and resolute explanation attendant on the tale. It was friendship melting into love.

The relation into which they now entered was an extremely happy one. Both held the same views on marriage, yet both felt the need of being inconsistent. It should be in their opinion apart from and independent of forms, yet for the sake of the child who was to be born, and for the sake of society, the ceremony took place at

Old St. Pancras Church on March 29, 1797. It was characteristic of Godwin that he did not notice the circumstance in his minute and careful diary, so wholly did he regard it as superfluous, the marriage having been binding on his heart and conscience long before.

The first intimation of the marriage was made to Miss Hayes, in the following letter:

April 10.

My fair neighbour desires me to announce to you a piece of news, which it is consonant to the regard that she and I entertain for you, you should rather learn from us than from any other quarter. She bids me remind you of the earnest way in which you pressed me to prevail upon her to change her name, and she directs me to add, that it has happened to me, like many other disputants, to be entrapped in my own toils: in short, that we found that there was no way so obvious for her to drop the name of Imlay, as to assume the name of Godwin. Mrs. Godwin—who the devil is that?—will be glad to see you at No. 29, Polygon, Somers Town, whenever you are inclined to favour her with a call.

And now Mary Wollstonecraft had a season of real calm in her stormy life. Godwin for once only in his life was stirred by a real passion, and his admiration for his wife equalled his affection. The very slight clouds which arose now and then were of a transient character, and sprang from Mary Wollstonecraft's excessive sensitiveness and eager quickness of temper. These were, perhaps, occasionally tried by Godwin's confirmed bachelor habits, and also by the fact that he took *au pied de la lettre* all that she had said about the independence of women, when in truth she leant a good deal on the aid of others.

In some respects she was content to acquiesce in his bachelor ways; they adopted a singular device for their uninterrupted student life. Godwin's strong view of the possibility that people may weary of being always together, led him to take rooms in a house about twenty doors from that in the Polygon, Somers Town, which was their joint home. To this study he repaired as soon as he rose in the morning, rarely even breakfasting at the Polygon, and here also he often slept. Each was engaged in his and her own literary occupations, and they seldom met, unless they walked out together, till dinner-time each day.

> We agreed also (says Godwin) in condemning the notion that a man and his wife cannot visit in mixed society but in company with each other, and we rather sought occasions of deviating from than in complying with this rule.

When the marriage was declared, some time after it had taken place, it was cordially received by all but Mrs. Inchbald, one of Godwin's oldest friends. All else, the Lambs, Holcroft, Mrs. Reveley, Mr. Johnson, found that they had gained two friends, if they had only known one before, that the marriage had brought out the higher qualities of each.

But the brighter life was to last but a short time. In five months after the marriage was declared it ended unexpectedly and tragically. Mary had suffered so little when Fanny was born, that she was, perhaps, imprudent before the birth of her next child. Mary Godwin, afterwards Mrs. Shelley, was born at 20 minutes past 11, August 30, 1797. At first all seemed going on well, but fever set in, and in spite of the most untiring care of Dr. Fordyce, Sir Anthony Carlisle, and tender nurses among her friends, Mary Wollstonecraft Godwin died on September 10 at 20 minutes past 8 in the morning.

Miss Hayes, who had been with her, wrote thus to Mr. Hugh Skeys:

> Myself and Mrs. Fenwick were the two female friends that were with Mrs. Godwin during her last illness. Mrs. Fenwick attended her from the beginning of her confinement with scarcely any intermission. I was with her for the four last days of her life; and though I have had but little experience of scenes of this sort, yet I can confidently affirm that my imagination could never have pictured to me a mind so tranquil under affliction so great. . . . Her whole soul seemed to dwell with anxious fondness on her friends; and her affections, which were at all times more alive than perhaps those of any other human being, seemed to gather new disinterestedness upon this trying occasion. The attachment and regret of those who surrounded her seemed to increase every hour; and if her principles are to be judged of by what I saw of her death, I should say that no principles could be more conducive to calmness and consolation.

Miss Fenwick wrote to Everina Wollstonecraft in the same strain, and says:

It is not possible to describe the unremitting and devoted attentions of her husband. . . .

No woman was ever more happy in marriage than Mrs. Godwin. Who ever endured more anguish than Mr. Godwin endures? Her description of him in the very last moments of her recollection was, "He is the kindest, best man in the world."

It has often been noticed, so often that the subject is trite, how a vein of comedy is found in the deepest tragedies of life. This is exemplified in a remark of Godwin to his dying wife, too characteristic of that unsentimental materialist to be passed over. In one of Mary Wollstonecraft's last hours, when she was suffering acute agony, Mr. Basil Montagu ran to Dr. Carlisle, and returned before the physician with an anodyne which he administered himself, raising her in bed to give it. The medicine had an immediate effect, and she turned to her husband, who held her hand, with a sigh of relief, and said, "Oh, Godwin, I am in heaven."

But even at that moment Godwin declined to be entrapped into the admission that heaven existed, and he calmly replied, "You mean, my dear, that your physical sensations are somewhat easier."

How much he loved her is proved by her exquisite portrait, drawn by his hand, in his novel of *St. Leon*, where Marguerite, one of the sweetest characters in the fiction of that day, is unmistakably sketched from the recollection of the writer's married life.

Mary Godwin was buried where she had been married, at Old St. Pancras. This was then a quiet, almost a country churchyard, with its pretty Norman church embowered in trees. A large weeping willow shadowed the grave itself.

There sixteen years afterwards the child whose birth had proved so fatal to her mother used to take her books in the warm days of June to spend every hour she could call her own. Behind the drooping boughs she made her study, and found peace from a stepmother who never loved her, and a father whom his increasing difficulties and constitutional unfitness to have the charge of a warm-hearted, impulsive girl, made hard and unsympathising. There Shelley found her over her books, and their intimacy ripened till over her mother's resting-place Mary Godwin placed her hand in his, and linked her fortunes with his own. But that event belongs to another biography and another generation.

Old St. Pancras churchyard has seen strange vicissitudes. The Midland Railway broke in on its peace; and when I visited it some years ago to search for Mary Wollstonecraft's original grave, I thought I had seldom seen a place of the dead so desecrated. Once more the wilderness blossoms as the rose; it has become a public garden, well tended and fair.

But neither in its shame nor its reparation did Mary Wollstonecraft lie there. When the railway invaded the spot, and Godwin had lain some years by his wife's side, their grandson, Sir Percy Shelley, removed their remains to Bournemouth churchyard to the grave where he had laid his mother. There, on a sunny bank sloping to the west, among the rose-wreathed crosses of many who have died in more orthodox beliefs, lie those who at least might each of them have said:

Write me as one who loves his fellow-men.

It is always idle to speculate on what might have been. Yet fancy will sometimes enjoy idleness, and it is difficult not to think for a moment on those two lives of Godwin and his wife, one shortened so untimeously, one so blighted. No one can doubt that each had a power to supplement and improve at once the life and genius of the other, and it is probable that Mary Godwin's calm faith might have softened her husband's ruggedness—his critical faculty would have matured her style, and pruned her luxuriant fancy. She had been more schooled in the actual work of life than he, and her experience might have saved her husband from the unfortunate pecuniary difficulties which were so great a burden on his later years. But this was not to be. She died in her prime, intellectual and physical, leaving to the daughter to whom she then gave birth a mingled inheritance of genius and sadness, of filial duty met by coldness at home, of deep wedded joys, and deep widowed sorrows. Her opinions have become in many particulars the commonplaces of our own day, while she who was first to proclaim what is now held innocently was forgotten or assailed.

C. K. P.

LETTERS TO IMLAY.

LETTER I.

[PARIS, *June,* ? 1793.]
Two o'clock.

MY DEAR LOVE,

After making my arrangements for our snug dinner to-day, I have been taken by storm, and obliged to promise to dine, at an early hour, with the Miss ———s, the only day they intend to pass here. I shall however leave the key in the door, and hope to find you at my fire-side when I return, about eight o'clock. Will you not wait for poor Joan? whom you will find better, and till then think very affectionately of her.

Yours truly,

MARY.

I am sitting down to dinner; so do not send an answer.

LETTER II.

[PARIS, *August*, 1793.]
Past Twelve o'clock, Monday Night.

I OBEY an emotion of my heart, which made me think of wishing thee, my love, good-night! before I go to rest, with more tenderness than I can to-morrow, when writing a hasty line or two under Colonel ———'s eye. You can scarcely imagine with what pleasure I anticipate the day, when we are to begin almost to live together; and you would smile to hear how many plans of employment I have in my head, now that I am confident my heart has found peace in your bosom. Cherish me with that dignified tenderness, which I have only found in you; and your own dear girl will try to keep under a quickness of feeling, that has sometimes given you pain. Yes, I will be *good*, that I may deserve to be happy; and whilst you love me, I cannot again fall into the miserable state which rendered life a burthen almost too heavy to be borne.

But, good-night! God bless you! Sterne says that is equal to a kiss—yet I would rather give you the kiss into the bargain, glowing with gratitude to Heaven, and affection to you. I like the word affection, because it signifies something habitual; and we are soon to meet, to try whether we have mind enough to keep our hearts warm.

I will be at the barrier a little after ten o'clock to-morrow. Yours,

———.

LETTER III.

[PARIS, *August*, 1793.]
Wednesday Morning.

You have often called me 'dear girl,' but you would now say good, did you know how very attentive I have been to the —— ever since I came to Paris. I am not however going to trouble you with the account, because I like to see your eyes praise me; and Milton insinuates that during such recitals, there are interruptions not ungrateful to the heart, when the honey that drops from the lips is not merely words.

Yet, I shall not (let me tell you before these people enter, to force me to huddle away my letter) be content with only a kiss of *duty*. You *must* be glad to see me, because you are glad, or I will make love to the shade of Mirabeau, to whom my heart continually turned, whilst I was talking with Madame ——, forcibly telling me that it will ever have sufficient warmth to love, whether I will or not, sentiment, though I so highly respect principle.

Not that I think Mirabeau utterly devoid of principles, far from it; and if I had not begun to form a new theory respecting men, I should, in the vanity of my heart, have imagined that I could have made something of his, it was composed of such materials. Hush! here they come! and love flies away in the twinkling of an eye, leaving a little brush of his wing on my pale cheeks.

I hope to see Dr. —— this morning; I am going to Mr. ——'s to meet him. ——, and some others, are invited to dine with us to-day; and to-morrow I am to spend the day with ——.

I shall probably not be able to return to St. Germains to-morrow; but it is no matter, because I must take a carriage, I have so many books that I immediately want, to take with me. On Friday then I shall expect you to dine with me. And, if you come a little before dinner, it is so long since I have seen you, you will not be scolded by yours affectionately,

MARY.

[This and the thirteen following letters were written during a separation of several months, during which Imlay was chiefly at Havre.]

LETTER IV.

[PARIS, *September*, 1793.]
Friday Morning.

A MAN, whom a letter from Mr. —— previously announced, called here yesterday for the payment of a draft; and, as he seemed disappointed at not finding you at home, I sent him to Mr. ——. I have since seen him, and he tells me he has settled the business.

So much for business! May I venture to talk a little longer about less weighty affairs? How are you? I have been following you all along the road this comfortless weather; for, when I am absent from those I love, my imagination is as lively as if my senses had never been gratified by their presence—I was going to say caresses —and why should I not? I have found out that I have more mind than you, in one respect; because I can, without any violent effort of reason, find food for love in the same object, much longer than you can. The way to my senses is through my heart; but, forgive me! I think there is sometimes a shorter cut to yours.

With ninety-nine men out of a hundred, a very sufficient dash of folly is necessary to render a woman *piquante*, a soft word for desirable; and, beyond these casual ebullitions of sympathy, few look for enjoyment by fostering a passion in their hearts. One reason, in short, why I wish my whole sex to become wiser, is, that the foolish ones may not, by their pretty folly, rob those whose sensibility keeps down their vanity, of the few roses that afford them some solace in the thorny road of life.

I do not know how I fell into these reflections, excepting one thought produced it—that these continual separations were necessary to warm your affection. Of late we are always separating. Crack! crack! and away you go!

This joke wears the sallow cast of thought; for, though I began to write cheerfully, some melancholy tears have found their way into my eyes, that linger there, whilst a glow of tenderness at my heart whispers that you are one of the best creatures in the world. Pardon then the vagaries of a mind that has been almost "crazed by care," as well as "crossed in hapless love," and bear with me a *little* longer! When we are settled in the country together, more duties will open before me, and my heart, which now, trembling into peace, is agitated by every emotion that awakens the remembrance of old griefs, will learn to rest on yours, with that dignity your character, not to talk of my own, demands.

Take care of yourself, and write soon to your own girl (you may add dear, if you please) who sincerely loves you, and will try to convince you of it, by becoming happier.

LETTER V.

[PARIS, *November*, 1793.]
Sunday Night.

I HAVE just received your letter, and feel as if I could not go to bed tranquilly without saying a few words in reply, merely to tell you that my mind is serene, and my heart affectionate.

Ever since you last saw me inclined to faint, I have felt some gentle twitches, which make me begin to think that I am nourishing a creature who will soon be sensible of my care. This thought has not only produced an overflowing of tenderness to you, but made me very attentive to calm my mind and take exercise, lest I should destroy an object, in whom we are to have a mutual interest, you know. Yesterday —do not smile!—finding that I had hurt myself by lifting precipitately a large log of wood, I sat down in an agony, till I felt those said twitches again.

Are you very busy?

* * * * *

So you may reckon on its being finished soon, though not before you come home, unless you are detained longer than I now allow myself to believe you will.

Be that as it may, write to me, my best love, and bid me be patient—kindly—and the expressions of kindness will again beguile the time, as sweetly as they have done to-night. Tell me also over and over again, that your happiness (and you deserve to be happy!) is closely connected with mine, and I will try to dissipate, as they rise, the fumes of former discontent, that have too often clouded the sunshine which you have endeavoured to diffuse through my mind. God bless you! Take care of yourself, and remember with tenderness your affectionate

       MARY.

I am going to rest very happy, and you have made me so. This is the kindest good-night I can utter.

LETTER VI.

[PARIS, *December*, 1793.]
Friday Morning.

I AM glad to find that other people can be unreasonable as well as myself, for be it known to thee, that I answered thy *first* letter the very night it reached me (Sunday), though thou couldst not receive it before Wednesday, because it was not sent off till the next day. There is a full, true, and particular account.

Yet I am not angry with thee, my love, for I think that it is a proof of stupidity, and, likewise, of a milk-and-water affection, which comes to the same thing, when the temper is governed by a square and compass. There is nothing picturesque in this straight-lined equality, and the passions always give grace to the actions.

Recollection now makes my heart bound to

thee; but, it is not to thy money-getting face, though I cannot be seriously displeased with the exertion which increases my esteem, or rather is what I should have expected from thy character. No; I have thy honest countenance before me—Pop—relaxed by tenderness; a little —little wounded by my whims; and thy eyes glistening with sympathy. Thy lips then feel softer than soft, and I rest my cheek on thine, forgetting all the world. I have not left the hue of love out of the picture—the rosy glow; and fancy has spread it over my own cheeks, I believe, for I feel them burning, whilst a delicious tear trembles in my eye, that would be all your own, if a grateful emotion, directed to the Father of nature, who has made me thus alive to happiness, did not give more warmth to the sentiment it divides. I must pause a moment.

Need I tell you that I am tranquil after writing thus? I do not know why, but I have more confidence in your affection, when absent, than present; nay, I think that you must love me, for, in the sincerity of my heart let me say it, I believe I deserve your tenderness, because I am true, and have a degree of sensibility that you can see and relish.

Yours sincerely,
MARY.

LETTER VII.

[PARIS, *December* 29, 1793.]
Sunday Morning.

YOU seem to have taken up your abode at Havre. Pray sir! when do you think of coming home? or, to write very considerately, when will business permit you? I shall expect (as the country people say in England) that you will make a *power* of money to indemnify me for your absence.

    *   *   *   *   *

Well! but, my love, to the old story—am I to see you this week, or this month? I do not know what you are about, for, as you did not tell me, I would not ask Mr. ——, who is generally pretty communicative.

I long to see Mrs. ——; not to hear from you,

so do not give yourself airs, but to get a letter from Mr. ——. And I am half angry with you for not informing me whether she had brought one with her or not. On this score I will cork up some of the kind things that were ready to drop from my pen, which has never been dipt in gall when addressing you; or, will only suffer an exclamation—"The creature!" or a kind look, to escape me, when I pass the slippers, which I could not remove from my *salle* door, though they are not the handsomest of their kind.

Be not too anxious to get money! for nothing worth having is to be purchased. God bless you.

Yours affectionately,
MARY.

LETTER VIII.

[PARIS, *December* 30, 1793.]
Monday Night.

MY BEST LOVE,

Your letter to-night was particularly grateful to my heart, depressed by the letters I received by ——, for he brought me several, and the parcel of books directed to Mr. —— was for me. Mr. ——'s letter was very long and very affectionate; but the account he gives me of his own affairs, though he obviously makes the best of them, has vexed me.

A melancholy letter from my sister Eliza has also harrassed my mind—that from my brother would have given me sincere pleasure; but for

*   *   *   *   *

There is a spirit of independence in his letter

that will please you; and you shall see it, when we are once more over the fire together. I think that you would hail him as a brother, with one of your tender looks, when your heart not only gives a lustre to your eye, but a dance of playfulness, that he would meet with a glow half made up of bashfulness, and a desire to please the ——, where shall I find a word to express the relationship which subsists between us? Shall I ask the little twitcher? But I have dropt half the sentence that was to tell you how much he would be inclined to love the man loved by his sister. I have been fancying myself sitting between you, ever since I began to write, and my heart has leaped at the thought! You see how I chat to you.

I did not receive your letter till I came home; and I did not expect it, for the post came in much later than usual. It was a cordial to me, and I wanted one.

Mr. —— tells me that he has written again and again. Love him a little! It would be a kind of separation, if you did not love those I love.

There was so much considerate tenderness in your epistle to-night, that, if it has not made you dearer to me, it has made me forcibly feel how very dear you are to me, by charming away half my cares.

Yours affectionately,
MARY.

LETTER IX.

[PARIS, *December* 31, 1793.]
Tuesday Morning.

THOUGH I have just sent a letter off, yet, as Captain —— offers to take one, I am not willing to let him go without a kind greeting, because trifles of this sort, without having any effect on my mind, damp my spirits; and you, with all your struggles to be manly, have some of the same sensibility. Do not bid it begone, for I love to see it striving to master your features; besides, these kind of sympathies are the life of affection; and why, in cultivating our understandings, should we try to dry up these springs of pleasure, which gush out to give a freshness to days browned by care!

The books sent to me are such as we may read together; so I shall not look into them till you return, when you shall read, whilst I mend my stockings.

Yours truly,
MARY.

LETTER X.

[PARIS, *January* 1, 1794.]
Wednesday Night.

As I have been, you tell me, three days without writing, I ought not to complain of two; yet, as I expected to receive a letter this afternoon, I am hurt; and why should I, by concealing it, affect the heroism I do not feel?

I hate commerce. How differently must ——'s head and heart be organized from mine! You will tell me that exertions are necessary: I am weary of them! The face of things, public and private, vexes me. The "peace" and clemency which seemed to be dawning a few days ago, disappear again. "I am fallen," as Milton said, "on evil days;" for I really believe that Europe will be in a state of convulsion during half a century at least. Life is but a labour of patience: it is always rolling a great stone up a hill; for, before a person can find a resting-place, imagining it is lodged, down it comes again, and all the work is to be done over anew!

Should I attempt to write any more, I could not change the strain. My head aches, and my heart is heavy. The world appears an "unweeded garden" where "things rank and vile" flourish best.

If you do not return soon—or, which is no such mighty matter, talk of it—I will throw my slippers out at window, and be off—nobody knows where.

Finding that I was observed, I told the good women, the two Mrs. ——s simply that I was with child: and let them stare! and ——, and ——, nay, all the world, may know it for aught I care! Yet I wish to avoid ——'s coarse jokes.

Considering the care and anxiety a woman must have about a child before it comes into the world, it seems to me, by a *natural right*, to belong to her. When men get immersed in the world, they seem to lose all sensations, excepting those necessary to continue or produce life! Are these the privileges of reason? Amongst the feathered race, whilst the hen keeps the young warm, her mate stays by to cheer her; but it is sufficient for man to condescend to get a child, in order to claim it. A man is a tyrant!

You may now tell me, that, if it were not for me, you would be laughing away with some honest fellows in London. The casual exercise of social sympathy would not be sufficient for me—I should not think such an heartless life worth preserving. It is necessary to be in good humour with you, to be pleased with the world.

Thursday Morning.

I was very low-spirited last night, ready to quarrel with your cheerful temper, which makes absence easy to you. And why should I mince the matter? I was offended at your not even mentioning it. I do not want to be loved like a goddess, but I wish to be necessary to you. God bless you!

LETTER XI.

[PARIS, *January*, 1794.]
Monday Night.

I HAVE just received your kind and rational letter, and would fain hide my face, glowing with shame for my folly. I would hide it in your bosom, if you would again open it to me, and nestle closely till you bade my fluttering heart be still, by saying that you forgave me. With eyes overflowing with tears, and in the humblest attitude, I entreat you. Do not turn from me, for indeed I love you fondly, and have been very wretched since the night I was so cruelly hurt by thinking that you had no confidence in me.

It is time for me to grow more reasonable, a few more of these caprices of sensibility would destroy me. I have, in fact, been very much indisposed for a few days past, and the notion that I was tormenting, or perhaps killing, a poor little animal, about whom I am grown anxious and tender, now I feel it alive, made me worse. My bowels have been dreadfully disordered, and everything I ate or drank disagreed with my stomach; still I feel intimations of its existence, though they have been fainter.

Do you think that the creature goes regularly to sleep? I am ready to ask as many questions as Voltaire's Man of Forty Crowns. Ah! do not continue to be angry with me! You perceive that I am already smiling through my tears. You have lightened my heart, and my frozen spirits are melting into playfulness.

Write the moment you receive this. I shall count the minutes. But drop not an angry word. I cannot now bear it. Yet, if you think I deserve a scolding (it does not admit of a question, I grant), wait till you come back, and then, if you are angry one day, I shall be sure of seeing you the next.

—— did not write to you, I suppose, because he talked of going to Havre. Hearing that I was ill, he called very kindly on me, not dreaming that it was some words that he incautiously let fall, which rendered me so.

God bless you, my love; do not shut your heart against a return of tenderness; and, as I now in fancy cling to you, be more than ever my support. Feel but as affectionate when you read this letter, as I did writing it, and you will make happy, your

MARY.

LETTER XII.

[PARIS, *January*, 1794.]
Wednesday Morning.

I WILL never, if I am not entirely cured of quarrelling, begin to encourage " quick-coming fancies," when we are separated. Yesterday, my love, I could not open your letter for some time; and, though it was not half as severe as I merited, it threw me into such a fit of trembling, as seriously alarmed me. I did not, as you may suppose, care for a little pain on my own account; but all the fears which I have had for a few days past, returned with fresh force. This morning I am better; will you not be glad to hear it? You perceive that sorrow has almost made a child of me, and that I want to be soothed to peace.

One thing you mistake in my character, and

imagine that to be coldness, which is just the contrary. For, when I am hurt by the person most dear to me, I must let out a whole torrent of emotions, in which tenderness would be uppermost, or stifle them altogether; and it appears to me almost a duty to stifle them when I imagine *that I am treated with coldness.*

I am afraid that I have vexed you, my own love. I know the quickness of your feelings—and let me, in the sincerity of my heart, assure you, there is nothing I would not suffer to make you happy. My own happiness wholly depends on you; and, knowing you, when my reason is not clouded, I look forward to a rational prospect of as much felicity as the earth affords, with a little dash of rapture into the bargain, if you will look at me, when we meet again, as you have sometimes greeted your humbled, yet most affectionate

MARY.

LETTER XIII.

[PARIS, *January*, 1794.]
Thursday Night.

I HAVE been wishing the time away, my kind love, unable to rest till I knew that my penitential letter had reached your hand; and this afternoon when your tender epistle of Tuesday gave such exquisite pleasure to your poor sick girl, her heart smote her to think that you were still to receive another cold one. Burn it also, my dearest; yet do not forget that even those letters were full of love; and I shall ever recollect that you did not wait to be mollified by my penitence, before you took me again to your heart.

I have been unwell, and would not, now I am recovering, take the journey, because I have been seriously alarmed and angry with myself, dreading continually the fatal consequence of my folly. But, should you think it right to remain at Havre, I shall find some opportunity in the course of a fortnight, or less perhaps, to come to you, and before then I shall be strong again. Yet do not be uneasy! I am really better, and never took such care of myself as I have done since you restored my peace of mind. The girl is come to warm my bed, so I will tenderly say, good night! and write a line or two in the morning.

Morning.

I wish you were here to walk with me this fine morning! yet your absence shall not prevent me. I have stayed at home too much; though, when I was so dreadfully out of spirits, I was careless of everything.

I will now sally forth (you will go with me in my heart) and try whether this fine bracing air will not give the vigour to the poor babe it had before I so inconsiderately gave way to the grief that deranged my bowels, and gave a turn to my whole system.

Yours truly,   MARY IMLAY.

LETTER XIV.

[PARIS, *February*, 1794.]
Saturday Morning.

THE two or three letters, which I have written to you lately, my love, will serve as an answer to your explanatory one. I cannot but respect your motives and conduct. I always respected them; and was only hurt, by what seemed to me a want of confidence, and consequently affection. I thought also, that if you were obliged to stay three months at Havre, I might as well have been with you. Well, well! what signifies what I brooded over. Let us now be friends!

I shall probably receive a letter from you to-day, sealing my pardon—and I will be careful not to torment you with my querulous humours, at least, till I see you again. Act as circumstances direct, and I will not enquire when they will permit you to return, convinced that you will hasten to your love when you have attained (or lost sight of) the object of your journey.

What a picture have you sketched of our fireside! Yes, my love, my fancy was instantly at work, and I found my head on your shoulder, whilst my eyes were fixed on the little creatures that were clinging about your knees. I did not absolutely determine that there should be six— if you have not set your heart on this round number.

I am going to dine with Mrs. ———. I have not been to visit her since the first day she came to Paris. I wish indeed to be out in the air as much as I can; for the exercise I have taken these two or three days past has been of such service to me, that I hope shortly to tell you that I am quite well. I have scarcely slept before last night, and then not much. The two Mrs. ——s have been very anxious and tender.

Yours truly,
MARY.

I need not desire you to give the colonel a good bottle of wine.

LETTER XV.

[PARIS, *February*, 1794.]
Sunday Morning.

I WROTE to you yesterday, my dearest; but, finding that the colonel is still detained (for his passport was forgotten at the office yesterday) I am not willing to let so many days elapse without your hearing from me, after having talked of illness and apprehensions.

I cannot boast of being quite recovered, yet I am (I must use my Yorkshire phrase; for, when my heart is warm, pop come the expressions of childhood into my head) so *lightsome*, that I think it will not *go badly with me*. And nothing shall be wanting on my part, I assure you; for I am urged on, not only by an enlivened affection for you, but by a new-born tenderness that plays cheerily round my dilating heart.

I was, therefore, in defiance of cold and dirt, out in the air the greater part of yesterday; and, if I get over this evening without a return of the fever that has tormented me, I shall talk no more of illness. I have promised the little creature, that its mother, who ought to cherish it, will not again plague it, and begged it to pardon me; and, since I could not hug either it or you to my breast, I have to my heart. I am afraid to read over this prattle, but it is only for your eye.

I have been seriously vexed to find that, whilst you were harrassed by impediments in your undertakings, I was giving you additional uneasiness. If you can make any of your plans answer, it is well; I do not think a *little* money inconvenient; but, should they fail, we will struggle cheerfully together—drawn closer by the pinching blasts of poverty.

Adieu, my love! Write often to your girl, and write long letters; for I not only like them for being longer, but because more heart steals into them; and I am happy to catch your heart whenever I can.

Yours sincerely,
MARY.

LETTER XVI.

[PARIS, *February*, 1794.]
Tuesday Morning.

I SEIZE this opportunity to inform you, that I am to set out on Thursday with Mr. ——, and hope to tell you soon (on your lips) how glad I shall be to see you. I have just got my passport, so I do not foresee any impediment to my reaching Havre, to bid you good night next Friday in my new apartment, where I am to meet you and love, in spite of care, to smile me to sleep, for I have not caught much rest since we parted.

You have, by your tenderness and worth, twisted yourself more artfully round my heart than I supposed possible. Let me indulge the thought that I have thrown out some tendrils to cling to the elm by which I wish to be supported. This is talking a new language for me! But, knowing that I am not a parasite-plant, I am willing to receive the proofs of affection, that every pulse replies to, when I think of being once more in the same house with you. God bless you!

Yours truly,
MARY.

LETTER XVII.

[PARIS, *February*, 1794.]
Wednesday Morning.

I ONLY send this as an *avant-coureur*, without jack-boots, to tell you that I am again on the wing, and hope to be with you a few hours after you receive it. I shall find you well and composed, I am sure; or, more properly speaking, cheerful. What is the reason that my spirits are not as manageable as yours? Yet, now I think of it, I will not allow that your temper is even, though I have promised myself, in order to obtain my own forgiveness, that I will not ruffle it for a long, long time—I am afraid to say never.

Farewell for a moment! Do not forget that I am driving towards you in person! My mind, unfettered, has flown to you long since, or rather has never left you.

I am well, and have no apprehension that I shall find the journey too fatiguing, when I follow the lead of my heart. With my face turned to Havre my spirits will not sink, and my mind has always hitherto enabled my body to do whatever I wished.

Yours affectionately,
MARY.

On March 11, after a brief union of about a fortnight, Imlay returned to Paris.

LETTER XVIII.

[1794.]
HAVRE, *Thursday Morning*, March 12.

WE are such creatures of habit, my love, that, though I cannot say I was sorry, childishly so, for your going, when I knew that you were to stay such a short time, and I had a plan of employment; yet I could not sleep. I turned to your side of the bed, and tried to make the most of the comfort of the pillow, which you used to tell me I was churlish about; but all would not do. I took, nevertheless, my walk before breakfast, though the weather was not inviting—and here I am, wishing you a finer day, and seeing you peep over my shoulder, as I write, with one of your kindest looks—when your eyes glisten, and a suffusion creeps over your relaxing features.

But I do not mean to dally with you this morning. So God bless you! Take care of yourself, and sometimes fold to your heart your affectionate

MARY.

LETTER XIX.

[HAVRE, *March*, 1794.]

Do not call me stupid for leaving on the table the little bit of paper I was to inclose. This comes of being in love at the fag-end of a letter of business. You know, you say, they will not chime together. I had got you by the fire-side, with the *gigot* smoking on the board, to lard your bare ribs, and behold, I closed my letter without taking the paper up, that was directly under my eyes! What had I got in them to render me so blind? I give you leave to answer the question, if you will not scold; for I am

    Yours most affectionately,

        MARY.

> Imlay returned to Havre shortly after the above letter was written. Mary gave birth to a daughter (Fanny) about the end of April, 1794. In August Imlay went alone to Paris, where he was joined by Mary in September, at the end of which month Imlay went on business to London.

LETTER XX.

[HAVRE, 1794.]
Sunday, August 17.

*   *   *   *   *

I HAVE promised —— to go with him to his country-house, where he is now permitted to dine—I, and the little darling, to be sure—whom I cannot help kissing with more fondness since you left us. I think I shall enjoy the fine prospect, and that it will rather enliven, than satiate my imagination.

I have called on Mrs. ——. She has the manners of a gentlewoman, with a dash of the easy French coquetry, which renders her *piquante*. But *Monsieur* her husband, whom nature never dreamed of casting in either the mould of a gentleman or lover, makes but an awkward figure in the foreground of the picture.

The Havrais are very ugly without doubt—and the house smelt of commerce from top to toe—so that his abortive attempt to display taste, only proved it to be one of the things not to be bought with gold. I was in a room a moment alone, and my attention was attracted by the *pendule*. A nymph was offering up her vows, before a smoking altar, to a fat-bottomed Cupid (saving your presence), who was kicking his heels in the air. Ah! kick on, thought I; for the demon of traffic will ever fright away the loves and graces that streak with the rosy beams of infant fancy the *sombre* day of life; whilst the imagination, not allowing us to see things as they are, enables us to catch a hasty draught of the running stream of delight, the thirst for which seems to be given only to tantalise us.

But I am philosophizing; nay, perhaps you will call me severe, and bid me let the square-headed money-getters alone. Peace to them! though none of the social sprites (and there are not a few, of different descriptions, who sport about the various inlets to my heart) gave me a twitch to restrain my pen.

I have been writing on, expecting poor —— to come; for, when I began, I merely thought of business; and, as this is the idea that most naturally associates with your image, I wonder I stumbled on any other.

Yet, as common life, in my opinion, is scarcely worth having, even with a *gigot* every day, and a pudding added thereunto, I will allow you to cultivate my judgment, if you will permit me to keep alive the sentiments in your heart, which may be termed romantic, because, the offspring of the senses and the imagination, they resemble the mother more than the father, when they produce the suffusion I admire. In spite of icy age, I hope still to see it, if you have not determined only to eat and drink, and be stupidly useful to the stupid.

Yours,
MARY.

LETTER XXI.

[1794.]
HAVRE, *August* 19, *Tuesday.*

I RECEIVED both your letters to-day. I had reckoned on hearing from you yesterday, therefore was disappointed, though I imputed your silence to the right cause. I intended answering your kind letter immediately, that you might have felt the pleasure it gave me; but —— came in, and some other things interrupted me; so that the fine vapour has evaporated, yet, leaving a sweet scent behind. I have only to tell you, what is sufficiently obvious, that the earnest desire I have shown to keep my place, or gain more ground in your heart, is a sure proof how necessary your affection is to my happiness. Still I do not think it false delicacy, or foolish pride, to wish that your attention to my happiness should arise *as much* from love, which is always rather a selfish passion, as reason—that is, I want you to promote my felicity, by seeking your own. For, whatever pleasure it may give me to discover your generosity of soul, I would not be dependent for your affection on the very quality I most admire. No; there are qualities in your heart which demand my affection; but unless the attachment appears to me clearly mutual, I shall labour only to esteem your character instead of cherishing a tenderness for your person.

I write in a hurry, because the little one, who has been sleeping a long time, begins to call for me. Poor thing! when I am sad, I lament that all my affections grow on me, till they become too strong for my peace, though they all afford me snatches of exquisite enjoyment. This for our little girl was at first very reasonable—more the effect of reason, a sense of duty, than feeling—now she has got into my heart and imagination, and when I walk out without her, her little figure is ever dancing before me.

You too have somehow clung round my heart. I found I could not eat my dinner in the great room, and, when I took up the large knife to carve for myself, tears rushed into my eyes. Do not, however, suppose that I am melancholy, for, when you are from me, I not only wonder how I can find fault with you, but how I can doubt your affection.

I will not mix any comments on the inclosed (it roused my indignation) with the effusion of tenderness, with which I assure you that you are the friend of my bosom, and the prop of my heart.

LETTER XXII.

[1794
HAVRE, *August* 20.

I WANT to know what steps you have taken respecting ——. Knavery always rouses my indignation. I should be gratified to hear that the law had chastised —— severely; but I do not wish you to see him, because the business does not now admit of peaceful discussion, and I do not exactly know how you would express your contempt.

Pray ask some questions about Tallien. I am still pleased with the dignity of his conduct. The other day, in the cause of humanity, he made use of a degree of address, which I admire, and mean to point out to you, as one of the few instances of address which do credit to the abilities of the man, without taking away from that confidence in his openness of heart, which is the true basis of both public and private friendship.

Do not suppose that I mean to allude to a little reserve of temper in you, of which I have sometimes complained! You have been used to a cunning woman, and you almost look for cunning. Nay, in *managing* my happiness, you now and then wounded my sensibility, concealing yourself till honest sympathy, giving you to me without disguise, lets me look into a heart, which my half-broken one wishes to creep into, to be revived and cherished. You have frankness of heart, but not often exactly that overflowing (*épanchement de cœur*), which becoming almost childish, appears a weakness only to the weak.

But I have left poor Tallien. I wanted you to enquire likewise whether, as a member declared in the Convention, Robespierre really maintained a *number* of mistresses. Should it prove so, I suspect that they rather flattered his vanity than his senses.

Here is a chatting, desultory epistle! But do not suppose that I mean to close it without mentioning the little damsel—who has been almost springing out of my arm—she certainly looks very like you; but I do not love her the less for that, whether I am angry or pleased with you.

Yours affectionately,

MARY.

[This is the first of a series of letters written during a separation of many months, to which no cordial meeting ever succeeded. They were sent from Paris, and bear the address of London.]

LETTER XXIII.

[PARIS, 1794.]
September 22.

I HAVE just written two letters, that are going by other conveyances, and which I reckon on your receiving long before this. I therefore merely write, because I know I should be disappointed at seeing anyone who had left you if you did not send a letter, were it ever so short, to tell me why you did not write a longer, and you will want to be told, over and over again, that our little Hercules is quite recovered.

Besides looking at me, there are three other things which delight her; to ride in a coach, to look at a scarlet waistcoat, and hear loud music

—yesterday, at the *fête,* she enjoyed the two latter; but, to honour J. J. Rousseau, I intend to give her a sash, the first she has ever had round her—and why not?—for I have always been half in love with him.

Well, this you will say is trifling—shall I talk about alum or soap? There is nothing picturesque in your present pursuits; my imagination, then, rather chooses to ramble back to the barrier with you, or to see you coming to meet me, and my basket of grapes. With what pleasure do I recollect your looks and words, when I have been sitting on the window, regarding the waving corn!

Believe me, sage sir, you have not sufficient respect for the imagination. I could prove to you in a trice that it is the mother of sentiment, the great distinction of our nature, the only purifier of the passions—animals have a portion of reason, and equal, if not more exquisite, senses; but no trace of imagination, or her offspring taste, appears in any of their actions.

The impulse of the senses, passions, if you will, and the conclusions of reason, draw men together; but the imagination is the true fire, stolen from heaven, to animate this cold creature of clay, producing all those fine sympathies that lead to rapture, rendering men social by expanding their hearts, instead of leaving them leisure to calculate how many comforts society affords.

If you call these observations romantic, a phrase in this place which would be tantamount to nonsensical, I shall be apt to retort, that you are embruted by trade and the vulgar enjoyments of life. Bring me then back your barrier-face, or you shall have nothing to say to my barrier-girl; and I shall fly from you, to cherish the remembrances that will ever be dear to me; for I am yours truly,

MARY.

LETTER XXIV.

[PARIS, 1794.]
Evening, September 23.

I HAVE been playing and laughing with the little girl so long, that I cannot take up my pen to address you without emotion. Pressing her to my bosom, she looked so like you (*entre nous,* your best looks, for I do not admire your commercial face), every nerve seemed to vibrate to the touch, and I began to think that there was something in the assertion of man and wife being one—for you seemed to pervade my whole frame, quickening the beat of my heart, and lending me the sympathetic tears you excited.

Have I anything more to say to you? No; not for the present—the rest is all flown away; and indulging tenderness for you, I cannot now complain of some people here, who have ruffled my temper for two or three days past.

Morning.

YESTERDAY B—— sent to me for my packet of letters. He called on me before; and I like him better than I did—that is, I have the same opinion of his understanding; but I think with you, he has more tenderness and real delicacy of feeling with respect to women, than are commonly to be met with. His manner, too, of speaking of his little girl, about the age of mine, interested me. I gave him a letter for my sister, and requested him to see her.

I have been interrupted. Mr. —— I suppose will write about business. Public affairs I do not descant on, except to tell you that they write now with great freedom and truth; and this liberty of the press will overthrow the Jacobins, I plainly perceive.

I hope you take care of your health. I

have got a habit of restlessness at night, which arises, I believe, from activity of mind; for, when I am alone, that is, not near one to whom I can open my heart, I sink into reveries and trains of thinking, which agitate and fatigue me.

This is my third letter; when am I to hear from you? I need not tell you, I suppose, that I am now writing with somebody in the room with me, and Marguerite is waiting to carry this to Mr. ———'s. I will then kiss the girl for you, and bid you adieu.

I desired you, in one of my other letters, to bring back to me your barrier-face—or that you should not be loved by my barrier-girl. I know that you will love her more and more, for she is a little affectionate, intelligent creature, with as much vivacity, I should think, as you could wish for.

I was going to tell you of two or three things which displease me here; but they are not of sufficient consequence to interrupt pleasing sensations. I have received a letter from Mr. ———.

I want you to bring —— with you. Madame S—— is by me, reading a German translation of your letters; she desires me to give her love to you, on account of what you say of the negroes.

   Yours most affectionately,
          MARY.

LETTER XXV.

[1794.]
PARIS, *September* 28.

I HAVE written to you three or four letters; but different causes have prevented my sending them by the persons who promised to take or forward them. The inclosed is one I wrote to go by B——; yet, finding that he will not arrive, before I hope, and believe, you will have set out on your return, I inclose it to you, and shall give it in charge to ——, as Mr. —— is detained, to whom also I gave a letter.

I cannot help being anxious to hear from you; but I shall not harrass you with accounts of inquietudes, or of cares that arise from peculiar circumstances. I have had so many little plagues here, that I have almost lamented that I left Havre. ——, who is at best a most helpless creature, is now, on account of her pregnancy, more trouble than use to me, so that I still continue to be almost a slave to the child. She indeed rewards me, for she is a sweet little creature; for, setting aside a mother's fondness (which, by the bye, is growing on me, her little intelligent smiles sinking into my heart), she has an astonishing degree of sensibility and observation. The other day by B——'s child, a fine one, she looked like a little sprite. She is all life and motion, and her eyes are not the eyes of a fool, I will swear.

I slept at St. Germain's, in the very room (if you have not forgot) in which you pressed me very tenderly to your heart. I did not forget to fold my darling to mine, with sensations that are almost too sacred to be alluded to.

Adieu, my love! Take care of yourself, if you wish to be the protector of your child, and the comfort of her mother.

I have received, for you, letters from ——. I want to hear how that affair finishes, though I do not know whether I have most contempt for his folly or knavery.

Your own,
MARY.

LETTER XXVI.

[PARIS, 1794.]
October 1.

IT is a heartless task to write letters without knowing whether they will ever reach you. I have given two to ———, who has been a-going, a-going every day for a week past; and three others, which were written in a low-spirited strain, a little querulous or so, I have not been able to forward by the opportunities that were mentioned to me. *Tant mieux!* you will say, and I will not say nay; for I should be sorry that the contents of a letter, when you are so far away, should damp the pleasure that the sight of it would afford—judging of your feelings by my own. I just now stumbled on one of the kind letters which you wrote during your last absence. You are, then, a dear affectionate creature, and I will not plague you. The letter which you chance to receive, when the absence is so long, ought to bring only tears of tenderness, without any bitter alloy, into your eyes.

After your return, I hope indeed that you will not be so immersed in business, as during the last three or four months past—for even money, taking into the account all the future comforts it is to procure, may be gained at too dear a rate, if painful impressions are left on the mind. These impressions were much more lively soon after you went away, than at present—for a thousand tender recollections efface the melancholy traces they left on my mind—and every emotion is on the same side as my reason, which always was on yours. Separated, it would be almost impious to dwell on real or imaginary imperfections of character. I feel that I love you; and, if I cannot be happy with you, I will seek it nowhere else.

My little darling grows every day more dear to me, and she often has a kiss when we are alone together, which I give her for you with all my heart.

I have been interrupted—and must send off my letter. The liberty of the press will produce a great effect here—the *cry of blood will not be vain!* Some more monsters will perish—and the Jacobins are conquered. Yet I almost fear the last flap of the tail of the beast.

I have had several trifling, teazing inconveniences here, which I shall not now trouble you with a detail of. I am sending —— back; her pregnancy rendered her useless. The girl I have got has more vivacity, which is better for the child.

I long to hear from you. Bring a copy of —— and —— with you.

—— is still here: he is a lost man. He really loves his wife, and is anxious about his children; but his indiscriminate hospitality and social feelings have given him an inveterate habit of drinking, that destroys his health, as well as renders his person disgusting. If his wife had more sense or delicacy, she might restrain him ; as it is, nothing will save him.

Yours most truly and affectionately,
MARY.

LETTER XXVII.

[PARIS, 1794.]
October 26.

MY DEAR LOVE,—I began to wish so earnestly to hear from you, that the sight of your letters occasioned such pleasurable emotions, I was obliged to throw them aside till the little girl and I were alone together; and this said little girl, our darling, is become a most intelligent little creature, and as gay as a lark, and that in the morning too, which I do not find quite so convenient. I once told you, that the sensations before she was born, and when she is sucking, were pleasant; but they do not deserve to be compared to the emotions I feel, when she stops to smile upon me, or laughs outright on meeting me unexpectedly in the street, or after a short absence. She has now the advantage of having two good nurses, and I am at present able to discharge my duty to her, without being the slave of it.

I have therefore employed and amused myself since I got rid of ——, and am making a progress in the language, amongst other things. I have also made some new acquaintance. I have almost *charmed* a judge of the tribunal, R——, who, though I should not have thought it possible, has humanity, if not *beaucoup d'esprit*. But let me tell you, if you do not make haste back, I shall be half in love with the author of the *Marseillaise*, who is a handsome man, a little too broad-faced or so, and plays sweetly on the violin.

What do you say to this threat? Why, *entre nous*, I like to give way to a sprightly vein when writing to you, that is, when I am pleased with you. "The devil," you know, is proverbially said to be "in a good humour when he is pleased." Will you not then be a good boy, and come back quickly to play with your girls?

but I shall not allow you to love the new-comer best.

* * * * *

My heart longs for your return, my love, and only looks for, and seeks happiness with you; yet do not imagine that I childishly wish you to come back before you have arranged things in such a manner that it will not be necessary for you to leave us soon again, or to make exertions which injure your constitution.

Yours most truly and tenderly,

MARY.

P.S.—You would oblige me by delivering the inclosed to Mr. ——, and pray call for an answer. It is for a person uncomfortably situated.

LETTER XXVIII.

[PARIS, 1794.]
December 26.

I HAVE been, my love, for some days tormented by fears, that I would not allow to assume a form. I had been expecting you daily, and I heard that many vessels had been driven on shore during the late gale. Well, I now see your letter, and find that you are safe; I will not regret, then, that your exertions have hitherto been so unavailing.

*   *   *   *   *

Be that as it may, return to me when you have arranged the other matters, which —— has been crowding on you. I want to be sure that you are safe, and not separated from me by a sea that must be passed. For, feeling that I am happier than I ever was, do you wonder at my sometimes dreading that fate has not done persecuting me? Come to me, my dearest friend, husband, father of my child! All these fond ties glow at my heart at this moment, and dim my eyes. With you an independence is desirable; and it is always within our reach, if affluence escapes us—without you the world again appears empty to me. But I am recurring to some of the melancholy thoughts that have flitted across my mind for some days past, and haunted my dreams.

My little darling is indeed a sweet child; and I am sorry that you are not here to see her little mind unfold itself. You talk of "dalliance," but certainly no lover was ever more attached to his mistress, than she is to me. Her eyes follow me everywhere, and by affection I have the most despotic power over her. She is all vivacity or softness—yes; I love her more than I thought I should. When I have been hurt at your stay, I have embraced her as my only comfort—when pleased with you, for looking and laughing like you; nay, I cannot, I find, long be angry with you, whilst I am kissing her for resembling you. But there would be no end to these details. Fold us both to your heart; for I am truly and affectionately

Yours,
MARY.

LETTER XXIX.

[PARIS, 1794.]
December 28.

* * * * *

I DO, my love, indeed sincerely sympathise with you in all your disappointments. Yet, knowing that you are well, and think of me with affection, I only lament other disappointments, because I am sorry that you should thus exert yourself in vain, and that you are kept from me.

——, I know, urges you to stay, and is continually branching out into new projects, because he has the idle desire to amass a large fortune, rather an immense one, merely to have the credit of having made it. But we who are governed by other motives, ought not to be led on by him. When we meet, we will discuss this subject. You will listen to reason, and it has probably occurred to you, that it will be better, in future, to pursue some sober plan, which may demand more time, and still enable you to arrive at the same end. It appears to me absurd to waste life in preparing to live.

Would it not now be possible to arrange your business in such a manner as to avoid the inquietudes, of which I have had my share since your departure? Is it not possible to enter into business as an employment necessary to keep the faculties awake, and (to sink a little in the expressions) the pot boiling, without suffering what must ever be considered as a secondary object, to engross the mind, and drive sentiment and affection out of the heart?

I am in a hurry to give this letter to the person who has promised to forward it with ——'s. I wish then, to counteract, in some measure, what he has doubtless recommended most warmly.

Stay, my friend, whilst it is *absolutely* necessary. I will give you no tenderer name, though it glows at my heart, unless you come the moment the settling the *present* objects permit. *I do not consent* to your taking any other journey, or the little woman and I will be off, the Lord knows where. But, as I had rather owe everything to your affection, and, I may add, to your reason (for this immoderate desire of wealth, which makes —— so eager to have you remain, is contrary to your principles of action), I will not importune you. I will only tell you that I long to see you, and, being at peace with you, I shall be hurt, rather than made angry, by delays. Having suffered so much in life, do not be surprised if I sometimes, when left to myself, grow gloomy, and suppose that it was all a dream, and that my happiness is not to last. I say happiness, because remembrance retrenches all the dark shades of the picture.

My little one begins to show her teeth, and use her legs. She wants you to bear your part in the nursing business, for I am fatigued with dancing her, and yet she is not satisfied; she wants you to thank her mother for taking such care of her, as you only can.

Yours truly,
MARY.

LETTER XXX.

[PARIS, 1794.]
December 29.

THOUGH I suppose you have later intelligence, yet, as —— has just informed me that he has an opportunity of sending immediately to you, I take advantage of it to inclose you

* * * * *

How I hate this crooked business! This intercourse with the world, which obliges one to see the worst side of human nature! Why cannot you be content with the object you had first in view when you entered into this wearisome labyrinth? I know very well that you have imperceptibly been drawn on; yet why does one project, successful or abortive, only give place to two others? Is it not sufficient to avoid poverty? I am contented to do my part; and, even here, sufficient to escape from wretchedness is not difficult to obtain. And, let me tell you, I have my project also, and if you do not soon return, the little girl and I will take care of ourselves; we will not accept any of your cold kindness—your distant civilities—no; not we.

This is but half jesting, for I am really tormented by the desire which —— manifests to have you remain where you are. Yet why do I talk to you? If he can persuade you, let him! for, if you are not happier with me, and your own wishes do not make you throw aside these eternal projects, I am above using any arguments, though reason as well as affection seems to offer them, if our affection be mutual, they will occur to you, and you will act accordingly.

Since my arrival here, I have found the German lady of whom you have heard me speak. Her first child died in the month; but she has another about the age of my Fanny, a fine little creature. They are still but contriving to live—earning their daily bread—yet, though they are but just above poverty, I envy them. She is a tender, affectionate mother, fatigued even by her attention. However, she has an affectionate husband in her turn to render her care light, and to share her pleasure.

I will own to you that, feeling extreme tenderness for my little girl, I grow sad very often when I am playing with her, that you are not here to observe with me how her mind unfolds, and her little heart becomes attached! These appear to me to be true pleasures, and still you suffer them to escape you, in search of what we may never enjoy. It is your own maxim to "live in the present moment." *If you do*, stay, for God's sake; but tell me the truth—if not, tell me when I may expect to see you, and let me not be always vainly looking for you, till I grow sick at heart.

Adieu! I am a little hurt. I must take my darling to my bosom to comfort me.

LETTER XXXI.

[PARIS, 1794.]
December 30.

SHOULD you receive three or four of the letters at once which I have written lately, do not think of Sir John Brute, for I do not mean to wife you. I only take advantage of every occasion, that one out of three of my epistles may reach your hands, and inform you that I am not of ——'s opinion, who talks till he makes me angry, of the necessity of your staying two or three months longer. I do not like this life of continual inquietude, and, *entre nous*, I am determined to try to earn some money here myself, in order to convince you that, if you choose to run about the world to get a fortune, it is for yourself, for the little girl and I will live without your assistance, unless you are with us. I may be termed proud; be it so, but I will never abandon certain principles of action.

The common run of men have such an ignoble way of thinking, that, if they debauch their hearts, and prostitute their persons, following perhaps a gust of inebriation, they suppose the wife, slave rather, whom they maintain, has no right to complain, and ought to receive the sultan, whenever he deigns to return, with open arms, though his have been polluted by half an hundred promiscuous amours during his absence.

I consider fidelity and constancy as two distinct things; yet the former is necessary to give life to the other, and such a degree of respect do I think due to myself, that, if only probity, which is a good thing in its place, brings you back, never return!—for if a wandering of the heart, or even a caprice of the imagination detains you, there is an end of all my hopes of happiness. I could not forgive it if I would.

I have gotten into a melancholy mood, you perceive. You know my opinion of men in general; you know that I think them systematic tyrants, and that it is the rarest thing in the world to meet with a man with sufficient delicacy of feeling to govern desire. When I am thus sad I lament that my little darling, fondly as I doat on her, is a girl. I am sorry to have a tie to a world that for me is ever sown with thorns.

You will call this an ill-humoured letter, when in fact, it is the strongest proof of affection I can give, to dread to lose you. —— has taken such pains to convince me that you must and ought to stay, that it has inconceivably depressed my spirits. You have always known my opinion. I have ever declared, that two people who mean to live together ought not to be long separated. If certain things are more necessary to you than me —search for them. Say but one word, and you shall never hear of me more. If not, for God's sake let us struggle with poverty — with any evil, but these continual inquietudes of business, which I have been told were to last but a few months, though every day the end appears more distant! This is the first letter in this strain that I have determined to forward to you; the rest lie by, because I was unwilling to give you pain, and I should not now write if I did not think that there would be no conclusion to the schemes, which demand, as I am told, your presence.

LETTER XXXII.

[PARIS, 1795.]
January 9.

I JUST now received one of your hasty *notes;* for business so entirely occupies you, that you have not time, or sufficient command of thought, to write letters. Beware! you seem to be got into a whirl of projects and schemes, which are drawing you into a gulf, that, if it do not absorb your happiness, will infallibly destroy mine.

Fatigued during my youth by the most arduous struggles, not only to obtain independence, but to render myself useful, not merely pleasure, for which I had the most lively taste,—I mean the simple pleasures that flow from passion and affection,—escaped me, but the most melancholy views of life were impressed by a disappointed heart on my mind. Since I knew you I have been endeavouring to go back to my former nature, and have allowed some time to glide away, winged with the delight which only spontaneous enjoyment can give. Why have you so soon dissolved the charm?

I am really unable to bear the continual inquietude which your and ——'s never-ending plans produce. This you may term want of firmness, but you are mistaken; I have still sufficient firmness to pursue my principle of action. The present misery, I cannot find a softer word to do justice to my feelings, appears to me unnecessary, and therefore I have not firmness to support it as you may think I ought. I should have been content, and still wish, to retire with you to a farm. My God! anything but these continual anxieties, anything but commerce, which debases the mind, and roots out affection from the heart.

I do not mean to complain of subordinate inconveniences; yet I will simply observe, that, led to expect you every week, I did not make the arrangements required by the present circumstances, to procure the necessaries of life. In order to have them, a servant, for that purpose only, is indispensable. The want of wood has made me catch the most violent cold I ever had; and my head is so disturbed by continual coughing, that I am unable to write without stopping frequently to recollect myself. This however, is one of the common evils which must be borne with—bodily pain does not touch the heart, though it fatigues the spirits.

Still, as you talk of your return, even in February, doubtingly, I have determined, the moment the weather changes, to wean my child. It is too soon for her to begin to divide sorrow! And as one has well said, "despair is a freeman," we will go and seek our fortune together.

This is not a caprice of the moment, for your absence has given new weight to some conclusions that I was very reluctantly forming before you left me. I do not choose to be a secondary object. If your feelings were in unison with mine, you would not sacrifice so much to visionary prospects of future advantage.

LETTER XXXIII.

[PARIS, 1795.]
January 15.

I WAS just going to begin my letter with the fag end of a song, which would only have told you, what I may as well say simply, that it is pleasant to forgive those we love. I have received your two letters, dated the 26th and 28th of December, and my anger died away. You can scarcely conceive the effect some of your letters have produced on me. After longing to hear from you during a tedious interval of suspense, I have seen a superscription written by you. Promising myself pleasure, and feeling emotion, I have laid it by me, till the person who brought it, left the room,—when, behold! on opening it, I have found only half-a-dozen hasty lines, that have damped all the rising affection of my soul.

Well, now for business—

  * * * * *

My animal is well; I have not yet taught her to eat, but nature is doing the business. I gave her a crust to assist the cutting of her teeth; and now she has two, she makes good use of them to gnaw a crust, biscuit, &c. You would laugh to see her; she is just like a little squirrel; she will guard a crust for two hours; and, after fixing her eye on an object for some time, dart on it with an aim as sure as a bird of prey—nothing can equal her life and spirits. I suffer from a cold; but it does not affect her. Adieu! Do not forget to love us—and come soon to tell us that you do.

LETTER XXXIV.

[PARIS, 1795.]
January 30.

FROM the purport of your last letters, I should suppose that this will scarcely reach you; and I have already written so many letters, that you have either not received, or neglected to acknowledge, I do not find it pleasant, or rather I have no inclination, to go over the same ground again. If you have received them, and are still detained by new projects, it is useless for me to say any more on the subject. I have done with it for ever; yet I ought to remind you that your pecuniary interest suffers by your absence.

* * * * *

For my part, my head is turned giddy, by

only hearing of plans to make money, and my contemptuous feelings have sometimes burst out. I therefore was glad that a violent cold gave me a pretext to stay at home, lest I should have uttered unseasonable truths.

My child is well, and the spring will perhaps restore me to myself. I have endured many inconveniences this winter, which I should be ashamed to mention, if they had been unavoidable. "The secondary pleasures of life," you say, "are very necessary to my comfort:" it may be so; but I have ever considered them as secondary. If therefore you accuse me of wanting the resolution necessary to bear the *common* evils of life, I should answer that I have not fashioned my mind to sustain them, because I would avoid them, cost what it would.

Adieu!

LETTER XXXV.

[PARIS, 1795.]
February 9.

THE melancholy presentiment has for some time hung on my spirits, that we were parted for ever; and the letters I received this day, by Mr. ——, convince me that it was not without foundation. You allude to some other letters, which I suppose have miscarried; for most of those I have got, were only a few hasty lines, calculated to wound the tenderness the sight of the superscriptions excited.

I mean not however to complain; yet so many feelings are struggling for utterance, and agitating a heart almost bursting with anguish, that I find it very difficult to write with any degree of coherence.

You left me indisposed, though you have

taken no notice of it; and the most fatiguing journey I ever had, contributed to continue it. However, I recovered my health; but a neglected cold, and continual inquietude during the last two months, have reduced me to a state of weakness I never before experienced. Those who did not know that the canker-worm was at work at the core, cautioned me about suckling my child too long. God preserve this poor child, and render her happier than her mother!

But I am wandering from my subject: indeed my head turns giddy, when I think that all the confidence I have had in the affection of others is come to this. I did not expect this blow from you. I have done my duty to you and my child; and if I am not to have any return of affection to reward me, I have the sad consolation of knowing that I deserved a better fate. My soul is weary, I am sick at heart; and, but for this little darling, I would cease to care about a life, which is now stripped of every charm.

You see how stupid I am, uttering declamation, when I meant simply to tell you, that I consider your requesting me to come to you, as merely dictated by honour. Indeed I scarcely understand you. You request me to come, and then tell me that you have not given up all thoughts of returning to this place.

When I determined to live with you, I was only governed by affection. I would share poverty with you, but I turn with affright from the sea of trouble on which you are entering. I have certain principles of action; I know what I look for to found my happiness on. It is not money. With you I wished for sufficient to procure the comforts of life, as it is, less will do. I can still exert myself to obtain the necessaries of life for my child, and she does not want more at present. I have two or three plans in my head to earn our subsistence; for do not suppose that, neglected by you, I will lie under obligations of a pecuniary kind to you! No; I would sooner submit to menial service. I wanted the support of your affection; that gone, all is over! I did not think, when I complained of ——'s contemptible avidity to accumulate money, that he would have dragged you into his schemes.

I cannot write. I inclose a fragment of a letter, written soon after your departure, and another which tenderness made me keep back when it was written. You will see then the sentiments of a calmer, though not a more determined moment. Do not insult me by saying, that "our being together is paramount to every other consideration!" Were it, you would not be running after a bubble, at the expense of my peace of mind.

Perhaps this is the last letter you will ever receive from me.

LETTER XXXVI.

[PARIS, 1795.]
February 10.

YOU talk of "permanent views and future comfort"—not for me, for I am dead to hope. The inquietudes of the last winter have finished the business, and my heart is not only broken, but my constitution destroyed. I conceive myself in a galloping consumption, and the continual anxiety I feel at the thought of leaving my child, feeds the fever that nightly devours me. It is on her account that I again write to you, to conjure you, by all that you hold sacred, to leave her here with the German lady you may have heard me mention! She has a child of the same age, and they may be brought up together, as I wish her to be brought up. I shall write more fully on the subject. To facilitate this, I shall give up my present lodgings, and go into the same house. I can live much cheaper there, which is now become an object. I have had 3,000 livres from ——, and I shall take one more, to pay my servant's wages, &c., and then I shall endeavour to procure what I want by my own exertions. I shall entirely give up the acquaintance of the Americans.

—— and I have not been on good terms for a long time. Yesterday he very unmanlily exulted over me, on account of your determination to stay. I had provoked it, it is true, by some asperities against commerce which have dropped from me when we have argued about the propriety of your remaining where you are; and it is no matter, I have drunk too deep of the bitter cup to care about trifles.

When you first entered into these plans, you bounded your views to the gaining of a thousand pounds. It was sufficient to have procured a farm in America, which would have been an independence. You find now that you did not know yourself, and that a certain situation in life is more necessary to you than you imagined —more necessary than an uncorrupted heart. For a year or two you may procure yourself what you call pleasure ; but, in the solitude of declining life, I shall be remembered with regret —I was going to say with remorse, but checked my pen.

As I have never concealed the nature of my connection with you, your reputation will not suffer. I shall never have a confident ; I am content with the approbation of my own mind ; and, if there be a searcher of hearts, mine will not be despised. Reading what you have written relative to the desertion of women, I have often wondered how theory and practice could be so different, till I recollected that the sentiments of passion, and the resolves of reason are very distinct. As to my sisters, as you are so continually hurried with business, you need not write to them ; I shall, when my mind is calmer. God bless you ! Adieu !

This has been such a period of barbarity and misery, I ought not to complain of having my share. I wish one moment that I had never heard of the cruelties that have been practised here, and the next, envy the mothers who have been killed with their children. Surely I had suffered enough in life, not to be cursed with a fondness, that burns up the vital stream I am imparting. You will think me mad: I would I were so, that I could forget my misery—so that my head or heart would be still.

LETTER XXXVII.

[PARIS, 1795.]
February 19.

WHEN I first received your letter, putting off your return to an indefinite time, I felt so hurt that I know not what I wrote. I am now calmer, though it was not the kind of wound over which time has the quickest effect; on the contrary, the more I think, the sadder I grow. Society fatigues me inexpressibly. So much so, that finding fault with everyone, I have only reason enough to discover that the fault is in myself. My child alone interests me, and, but for her, I should not take any pains to recover my health.

As it is, I shall wean her, and try if by that step (to which I feel a repugnance, for it is my only solace) I can get rid of my cough.

Physicians talk much of the danger attending any complaint on the lungs, after a woman has suckled for some months. They lay a stress also on the necessity of keeping the mind tranquil—and, my God! how has mine been harrassed! But whilst the caprices of other women are gratified, "the wind of heaven not suffered to visit them too rudely," I have not found a guardian angel, in heaven or on earth, to ward off sorrow or care from my bosom.

What sacrifices have you not made for a woman you did not respect! But I will not go over this ground. I want to tell you that I do not understand you. You say that you have not given up all thoughts of returning here—and I know that it will be necessary—nay is. I cannot explain myself; but if you have not lost your memory, you will easily divine my meaning. What! is our life then only to be made up of separations? and am I only to return to a country, that has not merely lost all charms for me, but for which I feel a repugnance that almost amounts to horror, only to be left there a prey to it!

Why is it so necessary that I should return? brought up here, my girl would be freer. Indeed, expecting you to join us, I had formed some plans of usefulness that have now vanished with my hopes of happiness.

In the bitterness of my heart, I could complain with reason, that I am left here dependent on a man, whose avidity to acquire a fortune has rendered him callous to every sentiment connected with social or affectionate emotions. With a brutal insensibility, he cannot help displaying the pleasure your determination to stay gives him, in spite of the effect it is visible it has had on me.

Till I can earn money, I shall endeavour to borrow some, for I want to avoid asking him continually for the sum necessary to maintain me. Do not mistake me, I have never been refused. Yet I have gone half a dozen times to the house to ask for it, and come away without speaking—you must guess why. Besides, I wish to avoid hearing of the eternal projects to which you have sacrificed my peace—not remembering—but I will be silent for ever——

LETTER XXXVIII.

[HAVRE, 1795.]
April 7.

HERE I am at Havre, on the wing towards you, and I write now only to tell you that you may expect me in the course of three or four days; for I shall not attempt to give vent to the different emotions which agitate my heart. You may term a feeling, which appears to me to be a degree of delicacy that naturally arises from sensibility, pride. Still I cannot indulge the very affectionate tenderness which glows in my bosom, without trembling, till I see, by your eyes, that it is mutual.

I sit, lost in thought, looking at the sea; and tears rush into my eyes when I find that I am cherishing any fond expectations. I have indeed been so unhappy this winter, I find it as difficult to acquire fresh hopes, as to regain tranquillity. Enough of this; lie still, foolish heart! But for the little girl, I could almost wish that it should cease to beat, to be no more alive to the anguish of disappointment.

Sweet little creature! I deprived myself of my only pleasure when I weaned her, about ten days ago. I am, however, glad I conquered my repugnance. It was necessary it should be done soon, and I did not wish to embitter the renewal of your acquaintance with her, by putting it off till we met. It was a painful exertion to me, and I thought it best to throw this inquietude with the rest, into the sack that I would fain throw over my shoulder. I wished to endure it alone, in short. Yet, after sending her to sleep in the next room for three or four nights, you cannot think with what joy I took her back again to sleep in my bosom!

I suppose I shall find you when I arrive, for I do not see any necessity for your coming to me. Pray inform Mr. —— that I have his little friend with me. My wishing to oblige him made me put myself to some inconvenience, and delay my departure, which was irksome to me, who have not quite so much philosophy, I would not for the world say indifference, as you. God bless you!

Yours truly,
MARY.

LETTER XXXIX.

[1795].
BRIGHTHELMSTONE, *Saturday, April* 11.

HERE we are, my love, and mean to set out early in the morning; and, if I can find you, I hope to dine with you to-morrow. I shall drive to ——'s hotel, where —— tells me you have been—and, if you have left it, I hope you will take care to be there to receive us.

I have brought with me Mr. ——'s little friend, and a girl whom I like to take care of our little darling, not on the way, for that fell to my share. But why do I write about trifles? or anything? are we not to meet soon? What does your heart say?

Yours truly,
MARY.

I have weaned my Fanny, and she is now eating away at the white bread.

LETTER XL.

[1795.]
LONDON, *Friday, May* 22.

I HAVE just received your affectionate letter, and am distressed to think that I have added to your embarrassments at this troublesome juncture, when the exertion of all the faculties of your mind appears to be necessary to extricate you out of your pecuniary difficulties. I suppose it was something relative to the circumstance you have mentioned, which made —— request to see me to-day, to *converse about a matter of great importance*. Be that as it may, his letter (such is the state of my spirits) inconceivably alarmed me, and rendered the last night as distressing, as the two former had been.

I have laboured to calm my mind since you left me. Still I find that tranquillity is not to be obtained by exertion; it is a feeling so different from the resignation of despair! I am, however, no longer angry with you, nor will I ever utter another complaint; there are arguments which convince the reason, whilst they carry death to the heart. We have had too many cruel explanations, that not only cloud every future prospect, but embitter the remembrances which alone give life to affection. Let the subject never be revived!

It seems to me that I have not only lost the hope, but the power of being happy. Every emotion is now sharpened by anguish. My soul has been shook, and my tone of feelings destroyed. I have gone out and sought for dissipation, if not amusement, merely to fatigue still more, I find, my irritable nerves——

My friend—my dear friend—examine yourself well. I am out of the question; for, alas! I am nothing, and discover what you wish to do—what will render you most comfortable—or, to be more explicit, whether you desire to live with me, or part for ever! When you can once ascertain it, tell me frankly, I conjure you! for, believe me, I have very involuntarily interrupted your peace.

I shall expect you to dinner on Monday, and will endeavour to assume a cheerful face to greet you; at any rate I will avoid conversations, which only tend to harrass your feelings, because I am most affectionately yours,

MARY.

LETTER XLI.

May 27, 1795.]
Wednesday.

I INCLOSE you the letter which you desired me to forward, and I am tempted very laconically to wish you a good morning, not because I am angry, or have nothing to say; but to keep down a wounded spirit. I shall make every effort to calm my mind, yet a strong conviction seems to whirl round in the very centre of my brain, which, like the fiat of fate, emphatically assures me that grief has a firm hold of my heart.

God bless you!

Yours sincerely,
MARY.

LETTER XLII.

[HULL, *May* 27, 1795.]
Wednesday, Two o'clock.

WE arrived here about an hour ago. I am extremely fatigued with the child, who would not rest quiet with anybody but me during the night; and now we are here in a comfortless, damp room, in a sort of a tomb-like house. This, however, I shall quickly remedy, for, when I have finished this letter, (which I must do immediately, because the post goes out early), I shall sally forth, and enquire about a vessel and an inn.

I will not distress you by talking of the depression of my spirits, or the struggle I had to keep alive my dying heart. It is even now too full to allow me to write with composure.— Imlay,—dear Imlay, am I always to be tossed about thus? shall I never find an asylum to rest *contented* in? How can you love to fly about continually, dropping down, as it were, in a new world—cold and strange—every other day! Why do you not attach those tender emotions round the idea of home, which even now dim my eyes? This alone is affection—every thing else is only humanity, electrified by sympathy.

I will write to you again to-morrow, when I know how long I am to be detained, and hope to get a letter quickly from you, to cheer yours sincerely and affectionately,

MARY.

Fanny is playing near me in high spirits. She was so pleased with the noise of the mail-horn, she has been continually imitating it. Adieu!

LETTER XLIII.

[HULL, *May* 28, 1795.]
Thursday.

A LADY has just sent to offer to take me to Beverley. I have then only a moment to exclaim against the vague manner in which people give information.

* * * * *

But why talk of inconveniences, which are in fact trifling, when compared with the sinking of the heart I have felt! I did not intend to touch this painful string. God bless you!

Yours truly,

MARY.

LETTER XLIV.

[HULL, 1795.]
Friday, June 12.

I HAVE just received yours dated the 9th, which I suppose was a mistake, for it could scarcely have loitered so long on the road. The general observations which apply to the state of your own mind, appear to me just, as far as they go; and I shall always consider it as one of the most serious misfortunes of my life, that I did not meet you, before satiety had rendered your senses so fastidious, as almost to close up every tender avenue of sentiment and affection that leads to your sympathetic heart. You have a heart, my friend, yet, hurried away by the impetuosity of inferior feelings, you have sought in vulgar excesses for that gratification which only the heart can bestow.

The common run of men, I know, with strong health and gross appetites, must have variety to banish *ennui*, because the imagination never lends its magic wand, to convert appetite into love, cemented by according reason. Ah! my friend, you know not the ineffable delight, the exquisite pleasure, which arises from an unison of affection and desire, when the whole soul and senses are abandoned to a lively imagination, that renders every emotion delicate and rapturous. Yes; these are emotions, over which satiety has no power, and the recollection of which, even disappointment cannot disenchant; but they do not exist without self-denial. These emotions, more or less strong, appear to me to be the distinctive characteristic of genius, the foundation of taste, and of that exquisite relish for the beauties of nature, of which the common herd of eaters and drinkers and *child-begetters* certainly have no idea. You will smile at an observation that has just occurred to me :— I consider those minds as the most strong and original whose imagination acts as the stimulus to their senses.

Well! you will ask what is the result of all this reasoning? Why, I cannot help thinking that it is possible for you, having great strength of mind, to return to nature, and regain a sanity of constitution, and purity of feeling, which would open your heart to me. I would fain rest there!

Yet, convinced more than ever of the sincerity and tenderness of my attachment to you, the involuntary hopes which a determination to live has revived, are not sufficiently strong to dissipate the cloud that despair has spread over futurity. I have looked at the sea, and at my child, hardly daring to own to myself the secret wish, that it might become our tomb; and that the heart, still so alive to anguish, might there be quieted by death. At this moment ten thousand complicated sentiments press for utterance, weigh on my heart, and obscure my sight.

Are we ever to meet again? and will you endeavour to render that meeting happier than the last? Will you endeavour to restrain your caprices, in order to give vigour to affection, and to give play to the checked sentiments that nature intended should expand your heart? I cannot indeed, without agony, think of your bosom's being continually contaminated; and bitter are the tears which exhaust my eyes, when I recollect why my child and I are forced to stray from the asylum, in which, after so many storms, I had hoped to rest, smiling at angry fate. These are not common sorrows; nor can you perhaps conceive how much active fortitude it requires to labour perpetually to blunt the shafts of disappointment.

Examine now yourself, and ascertain whether you can live in something like a settled style. Let our confidence in future be unbounded; consider whether you find it necessary to sacrifice me to what you term "the zest of life;" and, when you have once a clear view of your own motives, of your own incentive to action, do not deceive me!

The train of thoughts which the writing of this epistle awoke, makes me so wretched that I must take a walk, to rouse and calm my mind. But first, let me tell you, that, if you really wish to promote my happiness, you will endeavour to give me as much as you can of yourself. You have great mental energy, and your judgment seems to me so just that it is only the dupe of your inclination in discussing one subject.

The post does not go out to-day. To-morrow I may write more tranquilly. I cannot yet say when the vessel will sail in which I have determined to depart.

[The passage below in regard to a destroyed document, refers to some letters which were written under a purpose of suicide and not intended to be opened till afterwards.]

[HULL, *June* 13, 1795.]
Saturday Morning.

YOUR second letter reached me about an hour ago. You were certainly wrong in supposing that I did not mention you with respect; though, without my being conscious of it, some sparks of resentment may have animated the gloom of despair—Yes; with less affection, I should have been more respectful. However the regard which I have for you is so unequivocal to myself, I imagine that it must be sufficiently obvious to everybody else. Besides, the only letter I intended for the public eye was to ——, and that I destroyed from delicacy before you saw them, because it was only written (of course warmly in your praise) to prevent any odium being thrown on you.

I am harrassed by your embarrassments, and shall certainly use all my efforts to make the business terminate to your satisfaction in which I am engaged.

My friend—my dearest friend—I feel my fate united to yours by the most sacred principles of my soul, and the yearnings of—yes, I will say it—a true, unsophisticated heart.

Yours most truly,
MARY.

If the wind be fair, the captain talks of sailing on Monday; but I am afraid I shall be detained some days longer. At any rate, continue to write (I want this support) till you are sure I am where I cannot expect a letter; and, if any should arrive after my departure, a gentleman (not Mr. ——'s friend, I promise you) from whom I have received great civilities, will send them after me.

Do write by every occasion! I am anxious to hear how your affairs go on; and, still more, to be convinced that you are not separating yourself from us. For my little darling is calling papa, and adding her parrot word—Come, Come! And will you not come, and let us exert ourselves? I shall recover all my energy, when I am convinced that my exertions will draw us more closely together. One more adieu!

LETTER XLV.

[HULL, 1795.]
Sunday, June 14.

I RATHER expected to hear from you to-day. I wish you would not fail to write to me for a little time, because I am not quite well. Whether I have any good sleep or not, I wake in the morning in violent fits of trembling, and in spite of all my efforts, the child—everything—fatigues me, in which I seek for solace or amusement.

Mr. —— forced on me a letter to a physician of this place; it was fortunate, for I should otherwise have had some difficulty to obtain the necessary information. His wife is a pretty woman (I can admire, you know, a pretty woman, when I am alone,) and he an intelligent and rather interesting man. They have behaved to me with great hospitality; and poor Fanny was never so happy in her life as amongst their young brood.

They took me in their carriage to Beverley, and I ran over my favourite walks with a vivacity that would have astonished you. The town did not please me quite so well as formerly. It appeared so diminutive; and when I found that many of the inhabitants had lived in the same houses ever since I left it, I could not help wondering how they could thus have vegetated, whilst I was running over a world of sorrow, snatching at pleasure, and throwing off prejudices. The place where I at present am, is much improved; but it is astonishing what strides aristocracy and fanaticism have made since I resided in this country.

The wind does not appear inclined to change, so I am still forced to linger. When do you think that you shall be able to set out for France? I do not entirely like the aspect of your affairs, and still less your connections on either side of the water. Often do I sigh, when I think of your entanglements in business, and your extreme restlessness of mind. Even now I am almost afraid to ask you, whether the pleasure of being free does not overbalance the pain you felt at parting with me? Sometimes I indulge the hope that you will feel me necessary to you, or why should we meet again? but the moment after, despair damps my rising spirits, aggravated by the emotions of tenderness, which ought to soften the cares of life. God bless you!

Yours sincerely and affectionately,

MARY.

LETTER XLVI.

[HULL, 1795.]
June 15.

I WANT to know how you have settled with respect to ——. In short, be very particular in your account of all your affairs; let our confidence, my dear, be unbounded. The last time we were separated, was a separation indeed on your part. Now you have acted more ingenuously, let the most affectionate interchange of sentiments fill up the aching void of disappointment. I almost dread that your plans will prove abortive, yet, should the most unlucky turn send you home to us, convinced that a true friend is a treasure, I should not much mind having to struggle with the world again. Accuse me not of pride—yet sometimes, when nature has opened my heart to its author, I have wondered that you did not set a higher value on my heart.

Receive a kiss from Fanny, I was going to add, if you will not take one from me, and believe me yours

Sincerely,
MARY.

The wind still continues in the same quarter.

LETTER XLVII.

[HULL, *June* 16, 1795.]
Tuesday Morning.

THE captain has just sent to inform me that I must be on board in the course of a few hours. I wished to have stayed till to-morrow. It would have been a comfort to me to have received another letter from you. Should one arrive, it will be sent after me.

My spirits are agitated, I scarcely know why. The quitting England seems to be a fresh parting. Surely you will not forget me. A thousand weak forebodings assault my soul, and the state of my health renders me sensible to everything. It is surprising that in London, in a continual conflict of mind, I was still growing better, whilst here, bowed down by the despotic hand of fate, forced into resignation by despair,

I seem to be fading away—perishing beneath a cruel blight, that withers up all my faculties.

The child is perfectly well. My hand seems unwilling to add adieu! I know not why this inexpressible sadness has taken possession of me. It is not a presentiment of ill. Yet, having been so perpetually the sport of disappointment, having a heart that has been as it were a mark for misery, I dread to meet wretchedness in some new shape. Well, let it come, I care not! What have I to dread, who have so little to hope for! God bless you; I am most affectionately and sincerely yours,

MARY.

LETTER XLVIII.

[*June* 17, 1795.]
Wednesday Morning.

I WAS hurried on board yesterday about three o'clock, the wind having changed. But before evening it veered round to the old point; and here we are, in the midst of mists and water, only taking advantage of the tide to advance a few miles.

You will scarcely suppose that I left the town with reluctance, yet it was even so, for I wished to receive another letter from you, and I felt pain at parting, for ever perhaps, from the amiable family who had treated me with so much hospitality and kindness. They will probably send me your letter if it arrives this morning; for here we are likely to remain, I am afraid to think how long.

The vessel is very commodious, and the captain a civil, open-hearted, kind of man. There being no other passengers, I have the cabin to myself, which is pleasant; and I have brought a few books with me to beguile weariness; but I seem inclined rather to employ the dead moments of suspense in writing some effusions than in reading.

What are you about? How are your affairs going on? It may be a long time before you answer these questions. My dear friend, my heart sinks within me! Why am I forced thus to struggle continually with my affections and feelings? Ah! why are those affections and feelings the source of so much misery, when they seem to have been given to vivify my heart and extend my usefulness! But I must not dwell on this subject. Will you not endeavour to cherish all the affection you can for me? What am I saying? Rather forget me, if you can—if other gratifications are dearer to you. How is every remembrance of mine embittered by disappointment? What a world is this! They only seem happy who never look beyond sensual or artificial enjoyments. Adieu!

Fanny begins to play with the cabin-boy, and is as gay as a lark. I will labour to be tranquil; and am in every mood,

Yours sincerely,
MARY.

LETTER XLIX.

[*June* 18, 1795.]
Thursday.

HERE I am still, and I have just received your letter of Monday by the pilot, who promised to bring it to me, if we were detained, as he expected, by the wind. It is indeed wearisome to be thus tossed about without going forward. I have a violent head-ache, yet I am obliged to take care of the child, who is a little tormented by her teeth, because Marguerite is unable to do anything, she is rendered so sick by the motion of the ship as we ride at anchor.

These are, however, trifling inconveniences, compared with anguish of mind, compared with the sinking of a broken heart. To tell you the truth, I never suffered in my life so much from depression of spirits, from despair. I do not sleep, or if I close my eyes, it is to have the most terrifying dreams, in which I often meet you with different casts of countenance.

I will not, my dear love, torment you by dwelling on my sufferings, and will use all my efforts to calm my mind, instead of deadening it: at present it is most painfully active. I find I am not equal to these continual struggles, yet your letter this morning has afforded me some comfort, and I will try to revive hope. One thing let me tell you: when we meet again— surely we are to meet!—it must be to part no more. I mean not to have the sea between us; it is more than I can support.

The pilot is hurrying me. God bless you.

In spite of the commodiousness of the vessel, everything here would disgust my senses, had I nothing else to think of. "When the mind's free, the body's delicate;" mine has been too much hurt to regard trifles.

Yours most truly,
MARY.

LETTER L.

[*June* 20, 1795.]
Saturday.

THIS is the fifth dreary day I have been imprisoned by the wind, with every outward object to disgust the senses, and unable to banish the remembrances that sadden my heart.

How am I altered by disappointment! When going to Lisbon, ten years ago, the elasticity of my mind was sufficient to ward off weariness, and the imagination still could dip her brush in the rainbow of fancy, and sketch futurity in smiling colours. Now I am going towards the North in search of sunbeams! Will any ever warm this desolated heart? All nature seems to frown, or rather mourn with me. Everything is cold—cold as my expectations! Before I left the shore, tormented, as I now am, by the Northeast *chillers*, I could not help exclaiming, Give me, gracious Heaven! at least genial weather, if

I am never to meet the genial affection that still warms this agitated bosom, compelling life to linger there.

I am now going on shore with the captain, though the weather be rough, to seek for milk, &c., at a little village, and to take a walk—after which I hope to sleep—for confined here, surrounded by disagreeable smells, I have lost the little appetite I had; and I lie awake till thinking almost drives me to the brink of madness, only to the brink, for I never forget, even in the feverish slumbers I sometimes fall into, the misery I am labouring to blunt the sense of, by every exertion in my power.

Poor Marguerite still continues sick, and Fanny grows weary when the weather will not allow her to remain on deck.

I hope this will be the last letter I shall write from England to you; are you not tired of this lingering adieu?

Yours truly,

MARY.

LETTER LI.

[HULL, *June* 21, 1795.]
Sunday Morning.

THE captain last night, after I had written my letter to you intended to be left at a little village, offered to go to Hull to pass to-day. We had a troublesome sail; and now I must hurry on board again, for the wind has changed.

I half expected to find a letter from you here. Had you written one hap-hazard, it would have been kind and considerate; you might have known, had you thought, that the wind would not permit me to depart. These are attentions more grateful to the heart than offers of service. But why do I foolishly continue to look for them?

Adieu, adieu! My friend—your friendship is very cold—you see I am hurt. God bless you!

I may perhaps be, some time or other, independent in every sense of the word. Ah! there is but one sense of it of consequence. I will break or bend this weak heart, yet even now it is full.

Yours sincerely,
MARY.

The child is well; I did not leave her on board.

[A work published by Mary Wollstonecraft in 1796, under the title "Letters written during a Short Residence in Sweden, Norway, and Denmark," formed a part of the fourteen letters next following. All, however, that is here retained is the portion of the correspondence published by Godwin in 1798. The journal portion, however interesting, is a mere interruption to the personal narrative.]

LETTER LII.

[GOTHENBURG, 1795.]
June 27, Saturday.

I ARRIVED in Gothenburg this afternoon, after vainly attempting to land at Arendall. I have now but a moment, before the post goes out, to inform you we have got here; though not without considerable difficulty, for we were set ashore in a boat about twenty miles below.

What I suffered in the vessel I will not now descant upon, nor mention the pleasure I received from the sight of the rocky coast.

This morning, however, walking to join the carriage that was to transport us to this place, I fell, without any previous warning, senseless on the rocks, and how I escaped with life I can scarcely guess. I was in a stupor for a quarter of an hour; the suffusion of blood at last restored me to my senses; the contusion is great, and my brain confused. The child is well.

Twenty miles' ride in the rain, after my accident, has sufficiently deranged me; and here I could not get a fire to warm me, or anything warm to eat; the inns are mere stables; I must nevertheless go to bed. For God's sake, let me hear from you immediately, my friend! I am not well, and yet you see I cannot die.

Yours sincerely,
MARY.

LETTER LIII.

[GOTHENBURG, 1795.]
June 29.

I WROTE to you by the last post, to inform you of my arrival; and I believe I alluded to the extreme fatigue I endured on ship-board, owing to Marguerite's illness and the roughness of the weather. I likewise mentioned to you my fall, the effects of which I still feel, though I do not think it will have any serious consequences.

—— will go with me, if I find it necessary to go to Stromstad. The inns here are so bad, I was forced to accept an apartment in his house. I am overwhelmed with civilities on all sides, and fatigued with the endeavours to amuse me, from which I cannot escape.

My friend—my friend, I am not well; a

deadly weight of sorrow lies heavily on my heart. I am again tossed on the troubled billows of life; and obliged to cope with difficulties, without being buoyed up by the hopes that alone render them bearable. "How flat, dull, and unprofitable" appears to me all the bustle into which I see people here so eagerly enter! I long every night to go to bed, to hide my melancholy face in my pillow; but there is a canker-worm in my bosom that never sleeps.

LETTER LIV.

[SWEDEN, 1795.]
July 1.

I LABOUR in vain to calm my mind—my soul has been overwhelmed by sorrow and disappointment. Everything fatigues me; this is a life that cannot last long. It is you who must determine with respect to futurity; and, when you have, I will act accordingly—I mean, we must either resolve to live together or part for ever; I cannot bear these continual struggles. But I wish you to examine carefully your own heart and mind; and, if you perceive the least chance of being happier without me than with me, or if your inclination leans capriciously to that side, do not dissemble; but tell me frankly that you will never see me more. I will then adopt the plan I mentioned to you—for we must either live together, or I will be entirely independent.

My heart is so oppressed, I cannot write with precision. You know however, that what I so imperfectly express, are not the crude sentiments of the moment. You can only contribute to my comfort (it is the consolation I am in need of) by being with me; and, if the tenderest friendship is of any value, why will you not look to me for a degree of satisfaction that heartless affection cannot bestow?

Tell me then, will you determine to meet me at Basle? I shall, I should imagine, be at Hamburg before the close of August; and after you settle your affairs at Paris, could we not meet there?

God bless you!

Yours truly,

MARY.

Poor Fanny has suffered during the journey with her teeth.

LETTER LV.

[SWEDEN, 1795.]
July 3.

THERE was a gloominess diffused through your last letter, the impression of which still rests on my mind; though, recollecting how quickly you throw off the forcible feelings of the moment, I flatter myself it has long since given place to your usual cheerfulness.

Believe me (and my eyes fill with tears of tenderness as I assure you) there is nothing I would not endure in the way of privation, rather than disturb your tranquillity. If I am fated to be unhappy, I will labour to hide my sorrows in my own bosom; and you shall always find me a faithful, affectionate friend.

I grow more and more attached to my little girl, and I cherish this affection without fear, because it must be a long time before it can become bitterness of soul. She is an interesting creature. On ship-board, how often, as I gazed at the sea, have I longed to bury my troubled bosom in the less troubled deep; asserting with Brutus, "that the virtue I had followed too far, was merely an empty name!" and nothing but the sight of her—her playful smiles, which seemed to cling and twine round my heart—could have stopped me.

What peculiar misery has fallen to my share! To act up to my principles, I have laid the strictest restraint on my very thoughts. Yes; not to sully the delicacy of my feelings, I have reined in my imagination; and started with affright from every sensation, that stealing with balmy sweetness into my soul, led me to scent from afar the fragrance of reviving nature.

My friend, I have dearly paid for one conviction. Love, in some minds, is an affair of sentiment, arising from the same delicacy of perception (or taste) as renders them alive to the beauties of nature, poetry, &c., alive to the charms of those evanescent graces that are, as it were, impalpable—they must be felt, they cannot be described.

Love is a want of my heart. I have examined myself lately with more care than formerly, and find that to deaden is not to calm the mind. Aiming at tranquillity, I have almost destroyed all the energy of my soul—almost rooted out what renders it estimable. Yes, I have damped that enthusiasm of character, which converts the grossest materials into a fuel that imperceptibly feeds hopes, which aspire above common enjoyment. Despair, since the birth of my child, has rendered me stupid; soul and body seemed to be fading away before the withering touch of disappointment.

I am now endeavouring to recover myself; and such is the elasticity of my constitution, and the purity of the atmosphere here, that health unsought for begins to reanimate my countenance.

I have the sincerest esteem and affection for

you, but the desire of regaining peace (do you understand me?) has made me forget the respect due to my own emotions — sacred emotions, that are the sure harbingers of the delights I was formed to enjoy — and shall enjoy, for nothing can extinguish the heavenly spark.

Still, when we meet again, I will not torment you, I promise you. I blush when I recollect my former conduct, and will not in future confound myself with the beings whom I feel to be my inferiors. I will listen to delicacy, or pride.

LETTER LVI.

[SWEDEN, 1795.]
July 4.

I HOPE to hear from you by to-morrow's mail. My dearest friend! I cannot tear my affections from you—and, though every remembrance stings me to the soul, I think of you till I make allowance for the very defects of character that have given such a cruel stab to my peace.

Still, however, I am more alive than you have seen me for a long, long time. I have a degree of vivacity, even in my grief, which is preferable to the benumbing stupor that, for the last year, has frozen up all my faculties. Perhaps this change is more owing to returning health than to the vigour of my reason, for in spite of sadness (and surely I have had my share), the purity of this air, and the being continually out in it, for I sleep in the country every night, has made an alteration in my appearance that really surprises me. The rosy fingers of health already streak my cheeks—and I have seen a *physical* life in my eyes, after I have been climbing the rocks, that resembled the fond, credulous hopes of youth.

With what a cruel sigh have I recollected that I had forgotten to hope! Reason, or rather experience, does not thus cruelly damp poor Fanny's pleasures; she plays all day in the garden with ——'s children, and makes friends for herself.

Do not tell me that you are happier without us. Will you not come to us in Switzerland? Ah, why do not you love us with more sentiment?—why are you a creature of such sympathy, that the warmth of your feelings, or rather quickness of your senses, hardens your heart? It is my misfortune that my imagination is perpetually shading your defects, and lending you charms, whilst the grossness of your senses makes you (call me not vain) overlook graces in me, that only dignity of mind and the sensibility of an expanded heart can give. God bless you! Adieu.

LETTER LVII.

[SWEDEN, 1795.]
July 7.

I COULD not help feeling extremely mortified last post at not receiving a letter from you. My being at Stromstad was but a chance, and you might have hazarded it; and would a year ago.

I shall not, however, complain. There are misfortunes so great as to silence the usual expressions of sorrow. Believe me there is such a thing as a broken heart! There are characters whose very energy preys upon them; and who, ever inclined to cherish by reflection some passion, cannot rest satisfied with the common comforts of life. I have endeavoured to fly from myself, and launched into all the dissipation possible here, only to feel keener anguish, when alone with my child.

Still, could anything please me—had not disappointment cut me off from life, this romantic country, these fine evenings, would interest me. My God! can anything? and am I ever to feel alive only to painful sensations? But it cannot —it shall not last long.

The post is again arrived; I have sent to seek for letters, only to be wounded to the soul by a negative. My brain seems on fire. I must go into the air.

LETTER LVIII.

[LAURVIG, NORWAY, 1795.]
July 14.

I AM now on my journey to Tonsberg. I felt more at leaving my child than I thought I should; and, whilst at night I imagined every instant that I heard the half-formed sounds of her voice, I asked myself how I could think of parting with her for ever, of leaving her thus helpless?

Poor lamb! It may run very well in a tale, that "God will temper the winds to the shorn lamb!" but how can I expect that she will be shielded, when my naked bosom has had to brave continually the pitiless storm? Yes; I could add, with poor Lear, What is the war of elements to the pangs of disappointed affection, and the horror arising from a discovery of a breach of confidence that snaps every social tie!

All is not right somewhere! When you first knew me, I was not thus lost. I could still confide, for I opened my heart to you. Of this only comfort you have deprived me, whilst my happiness, you tell me, was your first object. Strange want of judgment!

I will not complain; but from the soundness of your understanding, I am convinced, if you give yourself leave to reflect, you will also feel that your conduct to me, so far from being generous, has not been just. I mean not to allude to factitious principles of morality; but to the simple basis of all rectitude. However I did not intend to argue. Your not writing is cruel—and my reason is perhaps disturbed by constant wretchedness.

Poor Marguerite would fain have accompanied me, out of tenderness; for my fainting, or rather convulsion, when I landed, and my sudden changes of countenance since, have alarmed her so much, that she is perpetually afraid of some accident. But it would have injured the child this warm season, as she is cutting her teeth.

I hear not of your having written to me at Stromstad. Very well! Act as you please—there is nothing I fear or care for! When I see whether I can, or cannot obtain the money I am come here about, I will not trouble you with letters to which you do not reply.

LETTER LIX.

[TONSBERG, NORWAY, 1795.]
July 18.

I AM here in Tonsberg, separated from my child—and here I must remain a month at least, or I might as well never have come.

*   *   *   *   *

I have begun ——, which will, I hope, discharge all my obligations of a pecuniary kind. I am lowered in my own eyes, on account of my not having done it sooner.

I shall make no further comments on your silence. God bless you!

LETTER LX.

[TONSBERG, 1795.]
July 30.

I HAVE just received two of your letters, dated the 26th and 30th of June; and you must have received several from me, informing you of my detention, and how much I was hurt by your silence.

*   *   *   *   *

Write to me then, my friend, and write explicitly. I have suffered, God knows, since I left you. Ah! you have never felt this kind of sickness of heart! My mind, however, is at present painfully active, and the sympathy I feel almost rises to agony. But this is not a subject of complaint; it has afforded me pleasure —and reflected pleasure is all I have to hope for—if a spark of hope be yet alive in my forlorn bosom.

I will try to write with a degree of composure. I wish for us to live together, because I want you to acquire an habitual tenderness for my poor girl. I cannot bear to think of leaving her alone in the world, or that she should only be protected by your sense of duty. Next to preserving her, my most earnest wish is not to disturb your peace. I have nothing to expect, and little to fear, in life. There are wounds that can never be healed—but they may be allowed to fester in silence without wincing.

When we meet again, you shall be convinced that I have more resolution than you give me credit for. I will not torment you. If I am destined always to be disappointed and unhappy, I will conceal the anguish I cannot dissipate; and the tightened cord of life or reason will at last snap, and set me free.

Yes; I shall be happy. This heart is worthy of the bliss its feelings anticipate—and I cannot even persuade myself, wretched as they have made me, that my principles and sentiments are not founded in nature and truth. But to have done with these subjects.

* * * * *

I have been seriously employed in this way since I came to Tonsberg; yet I never was so much in the air. I walk, I ride on horseback, row, bathe, and even sleep in the fields; my health is consequently improved. The child, Marguerite informs me, is well. I long to be with her.

Write to me immediately. Were I only to think of myself, I could wish you to return to me poor, with the simplicity of character, part of which you seem lately to have lost, that first attached to you.

Yours most affectionately,
MARY IMLAY.

I have been subscribing other letters, so I mechanically did the same to yours.

LETTER LXI.

[TONSBERG, 1795.]
August 5.

EMPLOYMENT and exercise have been of great service to me; and I have entirely recovered the strength and activity I lost during the time of my nursing. I have seldom been in better health; and my mind, though trembling to the touch of anguish, is calmer—yet still the same. I have, it is true, enjoyed some tranquillity, and more happiness here, than for a long, long time past. (I say happiness, for I can give no other appellation to the exquisite delight this wild country and fine summer have afforded me.) Still, on examining my heart, I find that it is so constituted, I cannot live without some particular affection—I am afraid not without a passion

—and I feel the want of it more in society, than in solitude.

* * * * *

Writing to you, whenever an affectionate epithet occurs, my eyes fill with tears, and my trembling hand stops; you may then depend on my resolution when with you. If I am doomed to be unhappy, I will confine my anguish in my own bosom; tenderness, rather than passion, has made me sometimes overlook delicacy; the same tenderness will in future restrain me.

God bless you!

LETTER LXII.

[TONSBERG, 1795.]
August 7.

AIR, exercise, and bathing, have restored me to health, braced my muscles, and covered my ribs, even whilst I have recovered my former activity. I cannot tell you that my mind is calm, though I have snatched some moments of exquisite delight, wandering through the woods, and resting on the rocks.

This state of suspense, my friend, is intolerable; we must determine on something, and soon; we must meet shortly, or part for ever. I am sensible that I acted foolishly, but I was wretched when we were together. Expecting too much, I let the pleasure I might have caught slip from me. I cannot live with you, I ought not—if you form another attachment. But I promise you, mine shall not be intruded on you. Little reason have I to expect a shadow of happiness, after the cruel disappointments that have rent my heart; but that of my child seems to depend on our being together. Still I do not wish you to sacrifice a chance of enjoyment for an uncertain good. I feel a conviction that I can provide for her, and it shall be my object —if we are indeed to part to meet no more. Her affection must not be divided. She must be a comfort to me—if I am to have no other— and only know me as her support. I feel that I cannot endure the anguish of corresponding with you—if we are only to correspond. No; if you seek for happiness elsewhere, my letters shall not interrupt your repose. I will be dead to you. I cannot express to you what pain it gives me to write about an eternal separation. You must determine—examine yourself. But, for God's sake! spare me the anxiety of uncertainty! I may sink under the trial; but I will not complain.

Adieu! If I had any thing more to say to you, it is all flown, and absorbed by the most tormenting apprehensions; yet I scarcely know what new form of misery I have to dread.

I ought to beg your pardon for having sometimes written peevishly, but you will impute it to affection, if you understand anything of the heart of

Yours truly,
MARY.

LETTER LXIII.

[TONSBERG, 1795.]
August 9.

FIVE of your letters have been sent after me from Stromstad. One, dated the 14th of July, was written in a style which I may have merited, but did not expect from you. However this is not a time to reply to it, except to assure you that you shall not be tormented with any more complaints. I am disgusted with myself for having so long importuned you with my affection.

My child is very well. We shall soon meet, to part no more, I hope—I mean I and my girl. I shall wait with some degree of anxiety till I am informed how your affairs terminate.

Yours sincerely,
MARY.

LETTER LXIV.

[GOTHENBURG, 1795.]
August 26.

I ARRIVED here last night, and with the most exquisite delight, once more pressed my babe to my heart. We shall part no more. You perhaps cannot conceive the pleasure it gave me, to see her run about, and play alone. Her increasing intelligence attaches me more and more to her. I have promised her that I will fulfil my duty to her, and nothing in future shall make me forget it. I will also exert myself to obtain an independence for her, but I will not be too anxious on this head.

I have already told you that I have recovered my health. Vigour, and even vivacity of mind, have returned with a renovated constitution. As for peace, we will not talk of it. I was not made, perhaps, to enjoy the calm contentment so termed.

*   *   *   *   *

You tell me that my letters torture you; I will not describe the effect yours have on me. I received three this morning, the last dated the 7th of this month. I mean not to give vent to the emotions they produced. Certainly you are right; our minds are not congenial. I have lived in an ideal world, and fostered sentiments that you do not comprehend, or you would not treat me thus. I am not, I will not be, merely an object of compassion—a clog, however light, to teaze you. Forget that I exist: I will never remind you. Something emphatical whispers me to put an end to these struggles. Be free —I will not torment, when I cannot please. I can take care of my child; you need not continually tell me that our fortune is inseparable, *that you will try to cherish tenderness* for me. Do no violence to yourself! When we are separated, our interest, since you give so much weight to pecuniary considerations, will be entirely divided. I want not protection without affection; and support I need not, whilst my faculties are undisturbed. I had a dislike to living in England; but painful feelings must give way to superior considerations. I may not be able to acquire the sum necessary to maintain my child and self elsewhere. It is too late to go to Switzerland. I shall not remain at [Hamburg], living expensively. But be not alarmed! I shall not force myself on you any more.

Adieu! I am agitated, my whole frame is convulsed, my lips tremble, as if shook by cold, though fire seems to be circulating in my veins.

God bless you!

LETTER LXV.

[COPENHAGEN, 1795.]
September 6.

I RECEIVED just now your letter of the 20th. I had written you a letter last night, into which imperceptibly slipt some of my bitterness of soul. I will copy the part relative to business. I am not sufficiently vain to imagine that I can, for more than a moment, cloud your enjoyment of life—to prevent even that, you had better never hear from me—and repose on the idea that I am happy.

Gracious God! It is impossible for me to stifle something like resentment, when I receive fresh proofs of your indifference. What I have suffered this last year is not to be forgotten! I have not that happy substitute for wisdom, insensibility—and the lively sympathies which bind me to my fellow creatures, are all of a painful kind. They are the agonies of a broken heart; pleasure and I have shaken hands.

I see here nothing but heaps of ruin, and only converse with people immersed in trade and sensuality.

I am weary of travelling, yet seem to have no home—no resting place to look to. I am strangely cast off. How often, passing through the rocks, I have thought, "But for this child, I would lay my head on one of them, and never open my eyes again!" With a heart feelingly alive to all the affections of my nature, I have never met with one softer than the stone that I would fain take for my last pillow. I once thought I had, but it was all a delusion. I meet with families continually, who are bound together by affection or principle, and, when I am conscious that I have fulfilled the duties of my station, almost to a forgetfulness of myself, I am ready to demand, in a murmuring tone, of Heaven, "Why am I thus abandoned?"

You say now

*   *   *   *   *

I do not understand you. It is necessary for you to write more explicitly, and determine on some mode of conduct. I cannot endure this suspense. Decide. Do you fear to strike another blow? We live together, or eternally apart! I shall not write to you again, till I receive an answer to this. I must compose my tortured soul before I write on indifferent subjects.

*   *   *   *   *

I do not know whether I write intelligibly, for my head is disturbed. But this you ought to pardon, for it is with difficulty frequently that I make out what you mean to say. You write, I suppose, at Mr. ———'s after dinner, when your head is not the clearest—and as for your heart, if you have one, I see nothing like the dictates of affection, unless a glimpse when you mention the child. Adieu!

LETTER LXVI.

[HAMBURG, 1795.]
September 25.

I HAVE just finished a letter to be given in charge to Captain ——. In that I complained of your silence, and expressed my surprise that three mails should have arrived without bringing a line for me. Since I closed it, I hear of another, and still no letter. I am labouring to write calmly—this silence is a refinement on cruelty. Had Captain —— remained a few days longer, I would have returned with him to England. What have I to do here? I have repeatedly written to you fully. Do you do the same, and quickly. Do not leave me in suspense. I have not deserved this of you. I cannot write, my mind is so distressed. Adieu!

* * * *

LETTER LXVII.

[HAMBURG, 1795.]
September 27.

WHEN you receive this, I shall either have landed, or be hovering on the British coast; your letter of the 18th decided me.

By what criterion of principle or affection you term my questions extraordinary and unnecessary, I cannot determine. You desire me to decide. I had decided. You must have had long ago two letters of mine, to the same purport, to consider. In these, God knows! there was but too much affection, and the agonies of a distracted mind were but too faithfully pourtrayed! What more then had I to say? The negative was to come from you. You had perpetually recurred to your promise of meeting me in the autumn. Was it extraordinary that I should demand a yes, or no? Your letter is written with extreme harshness, coldness I am accustomed to, in it I find not a trace of the tenderness of humanity, much less of friendship. I only see a desire to heave a load off your shoulders.

I am above disputing about words. It matters not in what terms you decide.

The tremendous power who formed this heart, must have foreseen that, in a world in which self-interest, in various shapes, is the principal mobile, I had little chance of escaping misery. To the fiat of fate I submit. I am content to be wretched; but I will not be contemptible. Of me you have no cause to complain, but for having had too much regard for you—for having expected a degree of permanent happiness, when you only fought for a momentary gratification.

I am strangely deficient in sagacity. Uniting myself to you, your tenderness seemed to make me amends for all my former misfortunes. On this tenderness and affection with that confidence did I rest!—but I leaned on a spear that has pierced me to the heart. You have thrown off a faithful friend, to pursue the caprices of the moment. We certainly are differently organized; for even now, when conviction has been stamped on my soul by sorrow, I can scarcely believe it possible. It depends at present on you, whether you will see me or not. I shall take no step, till I see or hear from you.

Preparing myself for the worst—I have determined, if your next letter be like the last, to write to Mr. Johnson to procure me an obscure lodging, and not to inform any body of my arrival. There I will endeavour in a few months to obtain the sum necessary to take me to France; from you I will not receive any more. I am not yet sufficiently humbled to depend on your beneficence.

Some people, whom my unhappiness has interested, though they know not the extent of it, will assist me to attain the object I have in view, the independence of my child. Should a peace take place, ready money will go a great way in France, and I will borrow a sum, which my industry *shall* enable me to pay at my leisure, to purchase a small estate for my girl. The assistance I shall find necessary to complete her education, I can get at an easy rate at Paris. I can introduce her to such society as she will like; and thus, securing for her all the chance for happiness, which depends on me, I shall die in peace, persuaded that the felicity which has hitherto cheated my expectation, will not always elude my grasp. No poor tempest-tossed mariner ever more earnestly longed to arrive at his port.

I shall not come up in the vessel all the way, because I have no place to go to. Captain —— will inform you where I am. It is needless to add, that I am not in a state of mind to bear suspense—and that I wish to see you, though it be for the last time.

LETTER LXVIII.

[DOVER, 1797.]
Sunday, October 4.

I WROTE to you by the packet, to inform you, that your letter of the 18th of last month, had determined me to set out with Captain —— ; but, as we sailed very quick, I take it for granted, that you have not received it.

You say, I must decide for myself. I have decided, that it was most for the interest of my little girl, and for my own comfort, little as I expect, for us to live together; and I even thought that you would be glad, some years hence, when the tumult of business was over, to repose in the society of an affectionate friend, and mark the progress of our interesting child, whilst endeavouring to be of use in the circle you at last resolved to rest in; for you cannot run about for ever.

From the tenour of your last letter however, I am led to imagine that you have formed some new attachment. If it be so, let me earnestly request you to see me once more, and immediately. This is the only proof I require of the friendship you profess for me. I will then decide, since you boggle about a mere form.

I am labouring to write with calmness; but the extreme anguish I feel, at landing without having any friend to receive me, and even to be conscious that the friend whom I most wish to see, will feel a disagreeable sensation at being informed of my arrival, does not come under the description of common misery. Every emotion yields to an overwhelming flood of sorrow, and the playfulness of my child distresses me. On her account, I wished to remain a few days here, comfortless as is my situation. Besides, I did not wish to surprise you. You have told me, that you would make any sacrifice to promote my happiness—and, even in your last unkind letter, you talk of the ties which bind you to me and my child. Tell me that you wish it, and I will cut this Gordian knot.

I now most earnestly intreat you to write to me, without fail, by the return of the post. Direct your letter to be left at the post-office, and tell me whether you will come to me here, or where you will meet me. I can receive your letter on Wednesday morning.

Do not keep me in suspense. I expect nothing from you, or any human being: my die is cast! I have fortitude enough to determine to do my duty; yet I cannot raise my depressed spirits, or calm my trembling heart. That being who moulded it thus, knows that I am unable to tear up by the roots the propensity to affection which has been the torment of my life—but life will have an end!

Should you come here (a few months ago I could not have doubted it) you will find me at ———. If you prefer meeting me on the road, tell me where.

     Yours affectionately,
         MARY.

LETTER LXIX.

[LONDON, *November*, 1795.]

I WRITE you now on my knees; imploring you to send my child and the maid with ——, to Paris, to be consigned to the care of Madame ——, Rue ——, Section de ——. Should they be removed, —— can give their direction.

Let the maid have all my clothes without distinction.

Pray pay the cook her wages, and do not mention the confession which I forced from her; a little sooner or later is of no consequence. Nothing but my extreme stupidity could have rendered me blind so long. Yet, whilst you assured me that you had no attachment, I thought we might still have lived together.

I shall make no comments on your conduct

or any appeal to the world. Let my wrongs sleep with me! Soon, very soon, I shall be at peace. When you receive this, my burning head will be cold.

I would encounter a thousand deaths, rather than a night like the last. Your treatment has thrown my mind into a state of chaos; yet I am serene. I go to find comfort, and my only fear is, that my poor body will be insulted by an endeavour to recall my hated existence. But I shall plunge into the Thames where there is the least chance of my being snatched from the death I seek.

God bless you! May you never know by experience what you have made me endure. Should your sensibility ever awake, remorse will find its way to your heart; and, in the midst of business and sensual pleasure, I shall appear before you, the victim of your deviation from rectitude.

LETTER LXX.

[LONDON, *November*, 1795.]
Sunday Morning.

I HAVE only to lament, that, when the bitterness of death was past, I was inhumanly brought back to life and misery. But a fixed determination is not to be baffled by disappointment; nor will I allow that to be a frantic attempt which was one of the calmest acts of reason. In this respect, I am only accountable to myself. Did I care for what is termed reputation, it is by other circumstances that I should be dishonoured.

You say, " that you know not how to extricate ourselves out of the wretchedness into which we have been plunged." You are extricated long since. But I forbear to comment. If I am condemned to live longer, it is a living death.

It appears to me that you lay much more stress on delicacy than on principle; for I am unable to discover what sentiment of delicacy would have been violated by your visiting a wretched friend, if indeed you have any friendship for me. But since your new attachment is the only sacred thing in your eyes, I am silent—Be happy! My complaints shall never more damp your enjoyment; perhaps I am mistaken in supposing that even my death could, for more than a moment. This is what you call magnanimity. It is happy for yourself, that you possess this quality in the highest degree.

Your continually asserting that you will do all in your power to contribute to my comfort, when you only allude to pecuniary assistance, appears to me a flagrant breach of delicacy. I want not such vulgar comfort, nor will I accept it. I never wanted but your heart—That gone, you have nothing more to give. Had I only poverty to fear, I should not shrink from life. Forgive me then, if I say, that I shall consider any direct or indirect attempt to supply my necessities, as an insult which I have not merited, and as rather done out of tenderness for your own reputation, than for me. Do not mistake me; I do not think that you value money, therefore I will not accept what you do not care for, though I do much less, because certain privations are not painful to me. When I am dead, respect for yourself will make you take care of the child.

I write with difficulty—probably I shall never write to you again. Adieu!

God bless you!

LETTER LXXI.

[LONDON, *November*, 1795.]
Monday Morning.

I AM compelled at last to say that you treat me ungenerously. I agree with you, that

*   *   *   *

But let the obloquy now fall on me. I fear neither poverty nor infamy. I am unequal to the task of writing, and explanations are not necessary.

*   *   *   *

My child may have to blush for her mother's want of prudence, and may lament that the rectitude of my heart made me above vulgar precautions; but she shall not despise me for meanness. You are now perfectly free. God bless you!

LETTER LXXII.

[LONDON, *November*, 1795.]
Saturday Night.

I HAVE been hurt by indirect enquiries, which appear to me not to be dictated by any tenderness to me. You ask, "If I am well or tranquil?" They who think me so, must want a heart to estimate my feelings by. I choose then to be the organ of my own sentiments.

I must tell you, that I am very mortified by your continually offering me pecuniary assistance; and, considering your going to the new house, as an open avowal that you abandon me, let me tell you that I will sooner perish than receive anything from you—and I say this at the moment when I am disappointed in my first attempt to obtain a temporary supply. But this even pleases me; an accumulation of disappointments and misfortunes seems to suit the habit of my mind.

Have but a little patience, and I will remove myself where it will not be necessary for you to talk—of course, not to think of me. But let me see, written by yourself—for I will not receive it through any other medium—that the affair is finished. It is an insult to me to suppose that I can be reconciled or recover my spirits ; but, if you hear nothing of me, it will be the same thing to you.

Even your seeing me, has been to oblige other people, and not to soothe my distracted mind.

LETTER LXXIII.

[LONDON, *November*, 1795.]
Thursday Afternoon.

MR. JOHNSON having forgot to desire you to send the things of mine which were left at the house, I have to request you to let Marguerite bring them to me.

I shall go this evening to the lodging; so you need not be restrained from coming here to transact your business. And, whatever I may think and feel, you need not fear that I shall publicly complain. No! If I have any criterion to judge of right and wrong, I have been most ungenerously treated: but, wishing now only to hide myself, I shall be silent as the grave in which I long to forget myself. I shall protect and provide for my child. I only mean by this to say, that you have nothing to fear from my desperation.

Farewell.

LETTER LXXIV.

[1795.]
LONDON, *November* 27.

THE letter, without an address, which you put up with the letters you returned, did not meet my eyes till just now. I had thrown the letters aside; I did not wish to look over a register of sorrow.

My not having seen it, will account for my having written to you with anger—under the impression your departure, without even a line left for me, made on me, even after your late conduct, which could not lead me to expect much attention to my sufferings. In fact, "the decided conduct which appeared to me so unfeeling," has almost overturned my reason; my mind is injured, I scarcely know where I am or what I do. The grief I cannot conquer (for some cruel recollections never quit me, banishing almost every other), I labour to conceal in total solitude. My life therefore is but an exercise of fortitude, continually on the stretch, and hope never gleams in this tomb, where I am buried alive.

But I meant to reason with you, and not to complain. You tell me, "that I shall judge more coolly of your mode of acting, some time hence." But is it not possible that *passion* clouds your reason as much as it does mine? And ought you not to doubt whether those principles are so "exalted," as you term them, which only lead to your own gratification? In other words, whether it would be just to have no principle of action but that of following your inclination, trampling on the affection you have fostered, and the expectations you have excited?

My affection for you is rooted in my heart. I know you are not what you now seem, nor will you always act or feel as you now do, though I may never be comforted by the change.

Even at Paris, my image will haunt you. You will see my pale face, and sometimes the tears of anguish will drop on your heart, which you have forced from mine.

I cannot write. I thought I could quickly have refuted all your *ingenious* arguments; but my head is confused. Right or wrong, I am miserable!

It seems to me that my conduct has always been governed by the strictest principles of justice and truth. Yet, how wretched have my social feelings and delicacy of sentiment rendered me! I have loved with my whole soul, only to discover that I had no chance of a return, and that existence is a burthen without it.

I do not perfectly understand you. If, by the offer of your friendship, you still only mean pecuniary support, I must again reject it. Trifling are the ills of poverty in the scale of my misfortunes. God bless you!

I have been treated ungenerously—if I understand what is generosity. You seem to me only to have been anxious to shake me off—regardless whether you dashed me to atoms by the fall. In truth, I have been rudely handled. *Do you judge coolly*, and I trust you will not continue to call those capricious feelings " the most refined," which would undermine not only the most sacred principles, but the affections which unite mankind. You would render mothers unnatural—and there would be no such thing as a father! If your theory of morals is the most " exalted," it is certainly the most easy. It does not require much magnanimity to determine to please ourselves for the moment, let others suffer what they will!

Excuse me for again tormenting you; my heart thirsts for justice from you; and whilst I recollect that you approved Miss ——'s conduct, I am convinced you will not always justify your own.

Beware of the deceptions of passion! It will

not always banish from your mind that you have acted ignobly, and condescended to subterfuge to gloss over the conduct you could not excuse. Do truth and principle require such sacrifices?

LETTER LXXV.

[1795.]
LONDON, *December* 8.

HAVING just been informed that —— is to return immediately to Paris, I would not miss a sure opportunity of writing, because I am not certain that my last by Dover has reached you.

Resentment, and even anger, are momentary emotions with me, and I wish to tell you so, that if you ever think of me, it may not be in the light of an enemy.

That I have not been used *well* I must ever feel; perhaps, not always with the keen anguish I do at present, for I began even now to write calmly, and I cannot restrain my tears.

I am stunned! Your late conduct still appears to me a frightful dream. Ah! ask yourself if you have not condescended to employ a little address, I could almost say cunning, unworthy of you? Principles are sacred things, and we never play with truth with impunity.

The expectation (I have too fondly nourished it) of regaining your affection, every day grows fainter and fainter. Indeed, it seems to me, when I am more sad than usual, that I shall never see you more. Yet you will not always forget me. You will feel something like remorse for having lived only for yourself, and sacrificed my peace to inferior gratifications. In a comfortless old age, you will remember that you had one disinterested friend, whose heart you wounded to the quick. The hour of recollection will come, and you will not be satisfied to act the part of a boy, till you fall into that of a dotard. I know that your mind, your heart, and your principles of action are all superior to your present conduct. You do, you must, respect me—and you will be sorry to forfeit my esteem.

You know best whether I am still preserving the remembrance of an imaginary being. I once thought that I knew you thoroughly, but now

I am obliged to leave some doubts that involuntarily press on me, to be cleared up by time.

You may render me unhappy, but cannot make me contemptible in my own eyes. I shall still be able to support my child, though I am disappointed in some other plans of usefulness, which I once believed would have afforded you equal pleasure.

Whilst I was with you, I restrained my natural generosity, because I thought your property in jeopardy. When I went to Sweden I requested you, *if you could conveniently*, not to forget my father, sisters, and some other people, whom I was interested about. Money was lavished away, yet not only my requests were neglected, but some trifling debts were not discharged, that now come on me. Was this friendship, or generosity? Will you not grant you have forgotten yourself? Still I have an affection for you. God bless you!

LETTER LXXVI.

[LONDON, *December*, 1795.]

As the parting from you for ever is the most serious event of my life, I will once expostulate with you, and call not the language of truth and feeling ingenuity!

I know the soundness of your understanding, and know that it is impossible for you always to confound the caprices of every wayward inclination with manly dictates of principle.

You tell me "that I torment you." Why do I? Because you cannot estrange your heart entirely from me, and you feel that justice is on my side. You urge "that your conduct was unequivocal." It was not. When your coolness has hurt me, with what tenderness have you endeavoured to remove the impression! and even before I returned to England, you took great pains to convince me that all my uneasiness was occasioned by the effect of a worn-out constitution; and you concluded your letter with these words, "Business alone has kept me from you. Come to any port, and I will fly down to my two dear girls with a heart all their own."

With these assurances, is it extraordinary that I should believe what I wished? I might, and did think that you had a struggle with old propensities; but I still thought that I and virtue should at last prevail. I still thought that you had a magnanimity of character, which would enable you to conquer yourself.

Imlay, believe me, it is not romance, you have acknowledged to me feelings of this kind. You could restore me to life and hope, and the satisfaction you would feel would amply repay you.

In tearing myself from you, it is my own heart I pierce; and the time will come, when you will lament that you have thrown away a heart, that, even in the moment of passion, you cannot despise. I would owe everything to your generosity, but, for God's sake, keep me no longer in suspense! Let me see you once more!

LETTER LXXVII.

[LONDON, *December*, 1795.]

YOU must do as you please with respect to the child. I could wish that it might be done soon, that my name may be no more mentioned to you. It is now finished. Convinced that you have neither regard nor friendship, I disdain to utter a reproach, though I have had reason to think that the "forbearance" talked of has not been very delicate. It is, however, of no consequence. I am glad you are satisfied with your own conduct.

I now solemnly assure you, that this is an eternal farewell. Yet I flinch not from the duties which tie me to life.

That there is "sophistry" on one side or other, is certain; but now it matters not on which. On my part it has not been a question of words. Yet your understanding or mine must be strangely warped, for what you term "delicacy," appears to me to be exactly the contrary. I have no criterion for morality, and have thought in vain, if the sensations which lead you to follow an ancle or step, be the sacred foundation of principle and affection. Mine has been of a very different nature, or it would not have stood the brunt of your sarcasms.

The sentiment in me is still sacred. If there be any part of me that will survive the sense of my misfortunes, it is the purity of my affections. The impetuosity of your senses may have led you to term mere animal desire, the source of principle; and it may give zest to some years to come. Whether you will always think so, I shall never know.

It is strange that, in spite of all you do, something like conviction forces me to believe that you are not what you appear to be.

I part with you in peace.

www.ingramcontent.com/pod-product-compliance
Lightning Source LLC
Chambersburg PA
CBHW031252250426
43672CB00029BA/2187